You and the Year 2000

Dan & Rick —

Best wishes to you
in the year 2000!

Jeff Shepard PhD

If you are interested in having Jeffrey Shepard speak to your group, please contact:

Lois Clifton
Indigo Ink Enterprises, Ltd.
267-B East 29th Street, Suite 104
Loveland, CO 80538

Phone: (970) 635-9738
Fax: (970) 593-1953
Email: loisc@indigo-ink.com
Web Site: www.indigo-ink.com

You and the Year 2000

A Practical Guide
for Things that Matter

Jeffrey M. Shepard, Ph.D.

Edited by Lois Clifton

Indigo Ink Publishing

Loveland

The publisher offers discounts on this book when ordered in bulk quantities. For more information, please contact the Corporate Sales Department:

        Phone: (970) 635-9738
        Fax: (970) 593-1953
        Email: corpsales@indigo-ink.com

Cover Design by Indigo Ink Enterprises, Ltd.
Book Design and Layout by JAGraphics (Julie Anne Geisert)
Printed by United Graphics, Incorporated

Foreword

One of the things that I learned in co-authoring *Chicken Soup for the Woman's Soul* and *Chicken Soup for the Mother's Soul* is that life continuously presents us with challenges and somehow we find a way to triumph and grow. Most of us deal with our struggles alone, or with the support of family and friends. It's rare to find a time of turmoil that would affect *all* of us simultaneously, but certainly one is on the horizon. It's called the year-2000 problem.

The year-2000 problem is a unique event. It's a technological phenomenon that will affect many of the computers that support nearly every aspect of business and government and the products and services they provide. Many of us aren't even aware of the work in progress right now in institutions and large companies to avoid or alleviate the problems. And even fewer of us are aware of the potential impact on our lives—individually and collectively.

But what's even more rare is to find ourselves with time to plan for and a process for dealing with this challenging period, and that's the real value of this book. The book is written about potential problems that will in some way affect *all* of us and about the risks to the basic things in life that matter to *each* of us. Family. Home. Health. Investments. It doesn't get any more basic than that.

Dr. Shepard explains the problems and risks involved with the year-2000 problem in a straightforward and candid way. More importantly, he provides specific tips that enable each of us to handle our own unique situation, helping relieve a lot of the stress and uncertainty we would otherwise face. It's a book that needs to be read. It's a book that *you* need to read.

Marci Shimoff

Table of Contents

Part One

Part Two

Introduction—How to Use This Book

The Future is something which everyone
reaches at the rate of sixty minutes an hour,
whatever he does, whoever he is.

C. S. Lewis, *The Screwtape Letters* (1942)

The year-2000 problem is being chronicled with increasing fervor in the nation's papers and magazines and on radio and television programs. During the past year, I watched the public awareness of the year-2000 issue grow from nothing to, for some, an apocalyptic fear. Today year-2000 issues are commanding major headlines. Yet, there are still a great number of people for whom the year-2000 problem has little meaning. Many people continue to have little understanding of the issue, thinking the problem refers to the biblical Armageddon or is relevant only to people who have home computers.

Many computer experts, government officials and reporters have worked hard to raise public consciousness of the year-2000 risks. However, this greater level of awareness has come at a price. In raising the call to arms, some of these people resorted to emotional appeal, frequently forfeiting reason. Because they focus on the most outrageous aspects of the year-2000 problem, some people have responded predictably—either running for the hills or denying the existence and scale of the problem. These responses, while not the most useful ones, are not uncommon forms of dealing with difficult issues.

Worry and the Year 2000

There are a lot of words and phrases that describe worry and its differing intensities: anxiety, fear, apprehension, concern, disquiet, uneasiness, misgiving, dread, distress, alarm, fright, horror, frenzy, hysteria, and panic. Worry and all its derivations is surprisingly common in our society where one in four Americans, about 65 million, qualify for an anxiety disorder diagnosis.

As a psychologist specializing in the treatment of certain anxiety disorders, I hear many similar descriptions in my office and see the resulting misery.

Many times, the worry comes from wanting, even insisting, that the world be different than the way it is. Often, people's concerns are about things over which they have little control.

Worry often stems from *uncertainty* about the future or fear that we don't have any *control* over our future. Helping you avoid this form of worry, fear, anticipation, whatever you want to call it, is what this book is about, specifically, the prevention of worry stemming from problems living in a world facing serious *technical difficulties*—over which we have little control but which could seriously affect the way we live.

You and the Year 2000

The year-2000 problem has the potential for being an event that causes tremendous apprehension. In fact, many businesses and agencies don't want the general populace to know there is such a thing as the year-2000 problem until it's been corrected. Certainly there are *many* groups working diligently to address their year-2000 computer problems. What has not been addressed adequately is how the year-2000 problem affects you and me.

I first became interested in the year-2000 problem as a small business professional. As I began evaluating the year-2000 problems in my office, it occurred to me that other clinics with which I worked closely probably had year-2000 problems, too. They did, and on a much greater scale than mine. And they were impacted by other businesses and government agencies that also had year-2000 problems, and so on. It didn't take long for me to realize that the year-2000 problem was one of *interconnectedness*—a problem where *your* year-2000 risks are *mine*.

This realization lead me to ask a lot of questions. Unfortunately, I found few answers. All of the information I found, with the singular exception of information about personal computers, was written for computer programmers and other technical people. This type of information did not provide answers to the questions I had about the potential impact of the year-2000 problem on my telephone service, bank and savings accounts, home heating supply, water supply, and even the stability of government agencies and departments. What was being done to address these concerns, and what could I do to reduce or eliminate personal risk?

It's time that some of these questions were asked and answered—for all of us that depend on the smooth operation of services that we tend to take for granted. To deal with the fear and worry that some of these questions and answers might create, it is important to have a plan or strategy for protecting yourself and those you care about.

What is in This Guide

This guide is offered to provide balance between the doomsayers and those who take too lightly the year-2000 problems we all face. The guide is divided into two parts:

Part I: The first part of the book provides information about the year-2000 challenges faced by the various businesses, services, products, and agencies that we depend on. Some of these challenges may seem overwhelming, but we need a basic understanding of these bigger issues to assess our own personal risk. Also in Part I you will find **Timely Tips**, factors to take into account in making your own year-2000 assessment and preparations. These points are general in nature, but are included to help you extend the information presented in the chapters to your daily life

Part II: The second part of the book is intended to help promote the development of strategies to avoid or minimize the impact that year-2000 problems might have on you and your family if businesses and government don't fix their problems—or if the fixes themselves cause problems. Part II is written with the recognition that everybody's situation is unique. We all have different life circumstances and, consequently, different levels of exposure to the year-2000 problem. There is no such thing as a single solution or strategy for everyone or every family—in this situation, one size does *not* fit all. Part II of the book, therefore, provides you with snapshots—scenarios about how typical individuals and families with different situations might approach the year -2000 problem. To help portray this, these snapshots are written as life stories—profiles of typical people who will soon be facing an atypical situation. Each circumstance was developed to help you identify situations or conditions that might have otherwise been overlooked.

Examine the profiles below. Do you recognize yourself? Do you know others that fit one of these profiles? Or a combination of profiles? The way these fictional people deal with the year-2000 problem could serve as a model for you.

Maggie

I am 37 years old, single, and own my own business. I like to think of myself as an entrepreneur and recognize that getting ahead sometimes means taking risks. My business is growing, and I have hired several employees to help out. Computers play a large role in my small business. We use them for keeping track of inventory, email, word processing, spreadsheets, and other business-related projects.

Financially, I consider myself to be middle class. I have some investments, including a 401K that is invested in stocks. I recently bought a home where I live in Southern California and am mortgaged to the hilt! My job is high stress, so I like to get away now and then. One of my favorite activities is camping in the mountains when I have the chance.

I originally grew up in New England, where my parents still live. Although in good health myself, I worry about my parents who are getting on in age. My father has a history of health problems, including a heart condition that's being treated with medications.

Dale and Patty

Patty and I have been married for nearly 35 years and are nearing retirement. We are fortunate to have invested well over the years, but find ourselves preparing for a life on fixed income. We have trimmed our cost of living to be more affordable, reducing our expenses to a mortgage payment, utilities, automobile fuel and maintenance expenses, and healthcare.

We own our home in the Northwest where we settled down many years ago and raised our children. Patty has been experiencing an increasing number of health problems in the past few years, and we find that healthcare and access to facilities is increasingly important to us.

John and Teresa

Teresa and I have been married for four years and have two young children. We just purchased a new home. In fact, it is still being built. We hope to move into it in just a couple of months.

I'm 35 years old and work as a salesman. My job requires frequent travel throughout the United States and overseas. During these trips I typically pay for my own expenses on credit cards and am reimbursed by the company afterwards. While on business trips, I rely on my portable computer which I use to download information from the company database. My second-favorite piece of equipment is my cell phone which I use to schedule meetings, talk with customers, and communicate with Teresa and the kids.

We are very close to our families and talk with them frequently. We also try to see them at least a couple times each year, especially around the holidays which have a special significance for us. We are concerned about the health of Teresa's mother who has been chronically ill for a number of years. She relies on government services, including Medicare and social security. She visits doctors often and, unfortunately, has made several trips to hospitals over the past few years for a variety of problems.

JoAnn and Derek

I'm JoAnn and I'm a single mom. My son, Derek, and I live in Chicago where I work as a secretary and where Derek goes to elementary school. We live in a high-rise apartment building and, to avoid traffic and save money, use the city's public transportation for most things.

A large part of my income goes for the basics, including child care. Derek's father helps out with child support, but even so, it seems I'm always stretched to the max. I'm going to school part time to get my college degree in business. Derek visits his father every other weekend, and they enjoy going to Cubs' games.

Additional Features in the Book

There are some additional features presented in each chapter to aid in your year-2000 preparation. These features provide quick, timely information for you and include:

- Points summarized at the beginning of each chapter to help familiarize you with information in the chapter
- Quick references to point to related information in other chapters
- Lots of tips to help get you going with your own year-2000 preparations
- Time Out! sections to provide historical or other interesting information, just because we all need a break from being too serious

Part One

Chapter 1

You and the Year 2000

In this chapter you will learn:

- What the year-2000 problem is and why it exists
- Why the year-2000 problem is a big deal and difficult to fix
- How the year-2000 problem affects business, government agencies, and you

In 1992, Mary Bandar of Winona, Minnesota was invited to join kindergarten classes when her name turned up among others identified in a database search for people born in "88"; at the time Bandar was 104.[1] "Boy, wouldn't those kids ever be surprised when they see me coming to school," replied Bandar.[2]

C.G. Blodgett, a living legend as an outdoorsman in New England, drives a car to his favorite fishing spots but almost quit this year when his insurance bill arrived. Classified as a youthful, high-risk driver, the 101-year-old's insurance premium had tripled.[3]

Moviegoers accustomed to paying with credit cards recently discovered a feature missing from nearly 100 of AMC Theatres' box offices: the ability to accept cards expiring in the year 2000 and later.[4]

A Michigan produce store has struggled with cash registers that freeze when customers use credit cards with year-2000 expiration dates. The store owners claimed that their computer, installed in 1995, had crashed more than 100 times, rendering 10 cash registers useless during the crashes.[5]

An automated Defense Logistics Agency system for the Department of Defense erroneously deactivated 90,000 inventoried items as the result of incorrect date calculations. According to the agency, if the problem had not been corrected (which took 400 work hours), the impact would have seriously hampered its mission to deliver materiel in a timely manner.[6]

What do a grandmother, fisherman, produce store, moviegoers, and the United States Department of Defense have in common? All have been impacted by a computer system's inability to handle date-related information correctly. This problem is simultaneously referred to as the year-2000 problem, millennium bug, or Y2K problem. As you can see from the examples above, the year-2000 problem is broad and encompasses many, if not most, areas of our lives because our society has become so computerized. Since the year-2000 problem can affect such a broad range of people and situations, it is in our best interest, as inventor Charles Kettering once said, to ". . . be concerned about the future because we will have to spend the rest of our lives there."

Scoping the Problem—It's About Time

During the '50s, '60s, and 70s, when business and government began to rely on computers, the storage capacity of computers was much more limited than it is today. Every little byte counted. Computer programmers realized that significant savings would result from storing fewer bytes, or individual pieces, of information. Since many computer programs use dates repeatedly, it made sense to abbreviate the year and use two digits instead of four. In all likelihood, most programmers probably never gave any thought to the impact of the millennium on computer systems, or believed that the systems they were working on would still be in operation in the year 2000. As a result, programming code, or software, on machines was almost universally standardized to use just two digits each to represent the day, month, *and* year—for example, 01/01/*99* instead of 01/01/*1999.* While people understand this abbreviated reference method and that double zeros would indicate the year 2000, computer systems do not.

In addition, many programs written for government and business organizations were custom made—written especially for them. This is in

Time Out!

January 1 has not always been considered the first day of the year. The first day of the new year has varied throughout time and by culture, ranging from Christmas day to as late as March 25. For example, from the twelfth century until 1752 when the Gregorian Calendar was adopted, the legal calendar in Great Britain considered the beginning of the year to be March 25.

Source:<www.magnet.ch/serendipity/hermetic/cal_stud/cal_art.htm>

contrast to the way most individuals buy software, choosing between several software packages at a store. These custom programs were modified over time, but in many, the two-digit date representation computer code was kept. As a result of these early practices, the computers running these software program could fail if corrections are not made—either ceasing to operate, corrupting data, or providing incorrect responses.

What Does This Have To Do With Me?

Want to understand the potential impact on you personally? Try this experiment. Most computers figure your age by subtracting the last two digits of the year you were born from the last two digits of the current date. So, to compute your age, you would subtract your birth year from the current year— say 1964, which happens to be my birth year, from 1998. Today, the computer systems would do the math, subtracting 64 from 98, and arrive at my accurate age—34. No problem.

But suppose the year is 2000. Remember, 2000 will be represented by only the last two digits, 00. So when the computer subtracts 64 from 00, it will compute my age as 64 (systems frequently take the absolute value, ignoring the fact the answer is really a negative 64). So if not corrected, in the year 2000 some systems will show that I've aged 30 years—in one year! Of course, if you were born prior to 1950, the years would be subtracted from your age. This may sound appealing—but what if you're near retirement and this error causes delays in receiving retirement benefits.

A Costly Little Problem to Fix

For business and government: The cost of storing records and data remains a major consideration today, especially for those companies and agencies that store millions and even billions of pieces of information—such as with insurance and banking, and federal and state agencies where the need to store data efficiently and cost effectively are critically important issues. Unfortunately, the strategy of reducing the year to two digits in order to save computer storage space, and thus money, is probably going to result in one of the most expensive bills in history. The problem, while seemingly simple, will require tremendous effort and expense to fix. Several articles have quoted the Gartner Group, a research firm regularly tracking the year-2000 problem, as estimating the worldwide price tag at about 600 *billion* dollars—a lot of money simply to ensure that everything will work exactly the same on January 1, 2000 as it did on December 31, 1999.

For You and Me: While most of us are not directly involved with large businesses and government agencies that rely on mainframes and PCs to monitor and regulate systems and databases, we are the ones who will be most impacted if year-2000 problems affecting those systems are not addressed. At risk, in varying degrees, are systems that control services and benefits that could be critical to survival and well being—ordinary things such as utilities, telecommunications, and transportation. For some of us, our health could also be at risk—if we don't understand the year-2000 problem and don't take ownership for assessing the risk to ourselves.

Try and plan a day where you don't come across modern technology in your life:

- Some household thermostats are computerized to determine the optimal time for heating or air conditioning.
- A visit to a doctor's office includes computerized scheduling and maintenance of your records, and, if you're using insurance, this visit could be billed electronically.
- Shopping at the grocery store includes buying merchandise that has electronic bar-code reading devices, and you can make your purchases via your credit or debit cards.
- Using the convenient ATM machine to obtain quick cash involves accessing your account information electronically.
- Filing an insurance claim involves accessing computerized information about your account and policy, which could include expiration dates embedded in your policy number.
- Monitoring or managing your 401K, IRA savings or stock market investments could involve electronic trading and information storing using date-sensitive devices.

The pervasive nature of the problem and an immovable deadline create a situation that is complex. This deadline simply can't be adjusted, altered, or changed. Business and government will either be prepared or they won't. Even a partial preparation means that *you* will be impacted by year-2000 related problems.

Complicating the Problem

To date, most of the solutions for the problem have been focused at the business and governmental level. To illustrate how long it takes to make some of these changes, the U.S. Social Security Administration (SSA) has been preparing for the year 2000 since 1989 and plans to have completed their preparations in the year 1998 or 1999. Eleven years to prepare! While most business don't have as complex a database as the SSA, there are, as of this writing, less than 500 days left to prepare. This doesn't allow sufficient time to organize, implement or test much except the most mission-critical systems. And this means that we, as well as the administration, are at risk for experiencing problems in the year 2000.

Something to Compare the Problem to

The United Parcel Service (UPS) strike in the fall of 1997 had a crippling effect on many small and large businesses and the individual citizen. UPS represents an important aspect of the business infrastructure. In many regards, the year-2000 problem is very similar. Imagine a goodly portion of the world's computer systems being rendered inoperable. What kind of impact would that have on businesses in your area, and possibly your day-to-day routine? Computers, whether they are the giant mainframes used in large government and business organizations, workstations, servers, or the millions of desktop

---

Over time, mistakes in calculating the Roman Calendar added up to 80 days. As a result the calendar bore little relationship to seasonal events. In the year 46 B.C., Julius Caesar ordered an adjustment to bring the calendar in line with the equinoxes. Caesar did this by adding two intercalations, or additions, to the calendar: 23 days following February 23 and 67 days before the end of November. This brought the number of days in the year 46 BC to 445. This became known as the year of confusion. Julius Caesar also added two months to the traditional ten in the Roman Calendar. This new calendar was called the Julian Calendar in his honor.

Time Out!

Source: <astro.nmsu.edu/~lhuber/leaphist.html> and <www.pip.dknet.dk/~pip10160/calendar.html>

PCs, are the backbone that allow the day-to-day operations and smooth functioning of our society.

Since the year-2000 problem stems principally from our use of computer technology, it is fair to anticipate that the areas most likely to experience problems are those that rely heavily on computer systems. Unfortunately, this includes almost every single business in the country, millions of households, not to mention every government agency from the Department of Defense to the Veteran's Administration. There is not a single major business or government agency that doesn't rely heavily on the use of computerized systems for its day-to-day functioning.

The fact is, any device that calculates time-sensitive information is potentially at risk of malfunctioning. And this problem isn't just a government or business problem. This information deals with the most critical aspects of your and your family's health and livelihood. This makes it your problem, too.

Recipe for Fixing the Problem

The advent of the year 2000 and fixing any problems that will occur is, in many ways, similar to the preparation of a big meal. Key to the success of the meal is the first stage: *the preparation.* For the meal, you must take stock of what you have and determine what ingredients are needed. It is also important to know when to start the preparations to ensure that everything is ready at the same time. And then, of course, there is the actual cooking. Starting too late would mean that you will have a lot of hungry guests waiting to be fed.

Preparing for the year-2000 problem requires a similar routine. Currently, there are thousands of people working hard to prepare their business computer systems. Much of the initial effort is involved in taking stock or creating an inventory of systems, determining what needs fixing, and understanding timing issues.

The feast itself is the second stage of the meal. The celebration. The big event. All the hard work comes down to a single point in time when, hopefully, you can enjoy the fruits of your labor. If you have prepared adequately, you will be free to enjoy the event and your guests.

This component, the meal itself, is analogous to the actual arrival of the year 2000. At this point, we are the hungry guests waiting to be served.

Cleaning up after the repast is the third and final component of a large meal, and the one that is the least enjoyable. There are lots of dishes to clean and things to put away. Rooms have to be straightened as well.

Similarly, there is probably going to be some cleanup after the year 2000 arrives, consisting of fixes that were either overlooked, incorrectly patched, or unanticipated. Some fixes can also create unanticipated problems, as you will learn later in the book.

Read about the IRS snafu in Chapter 11, *Government and the Year 2000.*

Disagreements Among the Cooks

The degree of preparation and the cleanup are hotly debated topics. Some believe that the *preparation stage* is going to require a lot of time, and that, even now, it is too late for many to get their kitchens in order. Others believe that year-2000 related problems have been exaggerated and that the preparations are not going to be difficult and time consuming.

Similarly, there is a lot of debate about the *cleanup stage*, the degree to which the year- 2000 computer problem will impact business, government, and society. As we get closer to the year 2000, the number of problems we are likely to experience is probably going to increase, reach their peak around the year 2000, then taper off over time. Estimates as to how quickly problems taper off is matter for speculation. Some believe that these problems could have long-term consequences, lasting for months or even years. Some have even speculated that governments may collapse as a result of the gridlock. On the other hand, others believe the problems to be minor and short lived. It is certain that some problems are going to occur well in advance to the year 2000. It is a myth to think that we will only begin experiencing problems after December 31, 1999.

Ultimately, nobody knows what might happen around the time of the year-2000 change. However, a cardinal rule in the hardware and software industry is that *bugs* create unknown and unexpected problems, including

---

The Julian period, not to be confused with the Julian Calendar, is the method used by astronomers for calculations. The Julian period covers a span of 7,980 years, and the current Julian period began on January 1, 4713 BC (on the Gregorian Calendar). The Julian period does not use years, but makes reference to the total number of days that have passed and assigns the letters JD, for Julian Day.

Time Out!

Source: <www.pip.dknet.dk/~pip10160/calendar.html>

---

problems that can't be fully anticipated. We do know that some problems are going to occur now, before the year 2000. Already, some people have had problems accessing ATM machines because the systems didn't know what to do with an expiration date in the next century. Other problems might not occur until well after the year 2000. For example, corrupted data in some government or insurance company databases could sit dormant for months or even years before coming to the fore. Speculation runs rampant, ranging from impending stock market collapse to minor or insignificant hassles. In any case, since we don't know what might happen, the best strategy is to be prepared.

The Last Word—*You* and the Year 2000

The purpose of this book is to serve as a guide in helping individuals—like you and me—protect themselves from the problems that will occur if the millions of computer systems in government and business don't meet the immovable deadline of January 1, 2000. The potential impact is too serious to not have a working knowledge of the problem and possible solutions—*and* a comprehension of your own level of risk.

The fact that the year-2000 problem is causing a lot of people to work hard to reduce its impact is not in question. The success they will have and the long-term consequences of these problems is the subject of hot debate. In large part, it will be up to you to decide whether or not you think the problem will be long lasting or of short duration.

It is also important to keep in mind that the degree of risk associated within any particular area is likely to change over time—the year-2000 problem is a moving target. For example, if banks and credit card companies successfully fix their computer systems, then perhaps you or members of your family won't need to carry cash to pay for that New Year's Eve night on the town.

But remember, the year-2000 problem is one of *interconnectedness*. Because one agency may be year-2000 compliant does not mean it won't have problems, especially if it works with an agency that did not get its problems fixed. The year-2000 problem is significant for a potential domino effect, and you will want to keep this in mind in considering your own year-2000 preparations.

Lastly, beware of individuals who try to scare you about issues related to the year 2000. Yes, these issues can be alarming. But this doesn't mean there aren't rational actions and preparations that can be made. It is very easy to fall into the trap of making decisions based on fear and worry. As a psychologist, I have found that many of the decisions that people later regret are the ones stemming from being anxious, angry, or hurt. This book will give you the information to make informed, sensible decisions about the year-2000 issues affecting you and your family.

We can't change the past and make the year-2000 problem go away by wishing, whining, or complaining. What *is* important are the choices we make *from this point forward*. The decisions and actions we take are what will determine the difference between being caught unaware and being prepared. So, let's begin! Let's take charge of our future and prepare for what could be a glorious new millennium!

Timely Tips—Guidelines for the Millennium

- Region of the country and local conditions may be important factors to consider for yourself and your family.
- Seasonal factors can be important. Remember, the brunt of year-2000 problems are likely to occur in January, a cold winter month for most of us.
- Age is an important consideration in making year-2000 related decisions. Older people and children are probably at higher risk because they are often more dependent on outside services.
- Health is a significant factor. In making plans, consider your personal health and/or the health of those important to you.
- Stay informed. Remember that the year-2000 problem is a moving target. Problems that exist today may be repaired. New areas of difficulty may be revealed, however. It is important to have current information as the countdown to the millennium proceeds.
- Think in terms of interrelationships and the domino effect, (e.g. the big picture), not solely in terms of isolated impacts. That is, if there is a year-2000 related power outage, what does this mean? Obviously, it means you need to find a way to keep warm, but it also means that you might have trouble finding fuel for the generator you bought because the gasoline pumps are electric and, therefore, won't pump fuel.

How big an impact do you prepare for? This is the most subjective question that you need to answer for yourself. Whether you prepare for a minimal, several-day problem, or month-long, year-long or longer-term problem is up to you and depends on the impact you think year-2000 related computer problems are going to create. This will be determined, in large part, by your comfort level with risk. The more risk averse you are, the safer you will want to be and the more you will want to prepare.

Time Out!

Different cultures used different standards for measuring time. For some, the sun was the major focus. Calendars using the sun, including the ancient Egyptian Calendar, are called solar calendars. The Islamic calendar, a lunar calendar, is based on the moon. Calendars using both the sun and the moon, such as the Hebrew calendar, are called lunisolar calendars.

Source: <astro.nmsu.edu/~lhuber/leaphist.html> and :<www.pip.dknet.dk/~pip10160/calendar.html>

---

[1] Hayes, Brian. 1995. Waiting for 01-01-00. *American Scientist*.

[2] Raven, Ed. 1993. Call for the Class of '88. *Risks Forum*, 14:44.

[3] Brian Hayes, Brian. 1995. Waiting for 01-01-00. *American Scientist.*

[4] Kalish. 1998. 2000 Crisis: It's Here. *San Diego Union-Tribune*.

[5] Wong, Wylie. 1997. Grocer Registers Year 2000 Suit. *Computerworld*, v31 n33 p6(1).

[6] General Accounting Office. 1997. Defense Computer: Issues Confronting DLA in Addressing Year 2000 Problems, page 4. Available at <http://www.gao.gov>

Chapter 2

Power and Water and the Year 2000

In this chapter you will learn:

- How the year-2000 problem could affect power production
- The risks to the production of power in your area of the country
- How the year-2000 problem puts nuclear power at particular risk for shutdown
- How the year-2000 problem could affect water supplies
- How embedded technologies could create problems with water availability and safety

Let there be light . . . and heat . . . and water . . .

Whether for two minutes or two weeks, nearly everybody at some point in their lives has experienced a power outage. Initially the loss of power can be exciting or challenging. But it doesn't take long before you begin to realize just how much you depend on, and take for granted, the availability of electricity. Sometimes the loss of power can lead to tragic results. Millions of people in the northeastern United States and Canada will recall the severe ice storms in January, 1998 that resulted in loss of power and at least 16 deaths.[1]

Thankfully, electricity—from production to distribution—is generally reliable. In most instances when the power does go out, it isn't out for very long. Longer outages are generally the result of damage to the infrastructure, as in the case of hurricanes, floods and tornadoes. In these situations power can be unavailable for an extended period of time. The question is, does the year 2000 represent one of those instances where the power supply could be lost? And if so, for how long?

Additional problems? Remember, the year 2000 will come in January—a bitterly cold month for most of the northern hemisphere. People's health, even lives, could be at risk if year-2000 problems affecting availability of power have not been investigated and addressed.

Electricity

Scoping the Problem—Controlling the Ebbs and Flows

Some year-2000 power-related concerns have already been reported, as in a June 2, 1997 *Newsweek* story. When Hawaiian Electric in Honolulu ran year-2000 compliance tests on its system, it found the system would not function. Hawaiian Electric now claims the system has been repaired; however, had the problem gone unaddressed after the year 2000, some customers could have lost power and others could have received power at a higher frequency, called a surge.

Many are seriously concerned about the year-2000 preparedness of the power industry as a whole. In June, 1998, the Senate Committee on the year 2000 reported the results of a survey[2] of the largest utility companies throughout the United States. The Committee concluded that:

- The pace of remedial efforts was too slow and the associated milestone dates were so distant that there was significant cause for concern.
- Despite substantial completion of initial assessments, firms were not confident that they had a complete and accurate picture of their present year-2000 compliance, making assurances of timely year-2000 compliance little more than a hope.
- Experts contend that the most difficult aspects of remediation are in the renovation and testing phases; most of the firms surveyed had not begun these phases of remediation.
- Utilities' ignorance of the year-2000 compliance of critical suppliers, vendors, and service providers and their lack of assurances from same created additional uncertainty for utility consumers.
- Since the firms tested are among the largest utilities in their fields with the most available resources, we [Senate Committee officials] are pessimistic about the implications of the rest of the utility sector.

Also disconcerting, the survey results indicated that while all firms reported checking with their suppliers and service providers, "... few of them received assurances of uninterrupted service and many are having difficulty obtaining responses to their inquiries. This creates some additional uncertainty for continuous utility service after the millennial date change."[3]

The power industry has a unique problem—once generated, electricity cannot be stored. Regrettably, there is no *national battery* storing excess energy for times of crisis. It is important, therefore, that everyone have an understanding of the challenges facing this sector. This chapter investigates year-2000 issues related to the many and varied components comprising the power industry, specifically, billing, power generation, regional consumption by source, the electric power grid, and water.

Regional Consumption by Source

Regional sources of power can differ dramatically. For example, if you are in the New England states, the light you may be using to read this book is probably coming from nuclear sources. Nuclear energy accounts for up to 40% of New England's power needs. However, if you are living in Seattle on the west coast of the United States, the power source used to heat your cup of Starbucks coffee more than likely comes from hydroelectric sources. If you are in the Midwest or mountain states, your electric power is derived primarily from coal.

Knowing the source of your power is important because the year-2000 risks for the various power sources differ. This means that at the millennium, some areas of the country may be at greater risk for power outages than others.

Failure of a single power generation plant, whether it uses coal, nuclear, natural gas, or hydroelectric sources, is not likely to cause widespread power

Percentage Total by Region and Energy Source

State/Region	Coal	Fuel Oil	Natural Gas	Nuclear Fuel	Hydroelectric
Total United States	57%	2%	9%	22%	11%
New England	23%	17%	12%	41%	6%
Middle Atlantic	43%	4%	6%	38%	9%
East North Central	76%	0%	0%	22%	0%
West North Central	75%	0%	1%	17%	6%
South Atlantic	60%	4%	6%	28%	2%
East South Central	70%	0%	2%	25%	8%
West South Central	49%	0%	34%	15%	1%
Mountain	70%	0%	4%	11%	15%
Pacific	4%	0%	12%	14%	68%
Alaska and Hawaii	2%	62%	26%	-	9%

Source: Information derived from Table 23, Sources of Energy for Electric Generation by State and Energy Source, 1996 Statistical Yearbook, Edison Electric Institute. Percentages may not add up to 100% due to rounding and non-inclusion of miscellaneous power resources.

Time Out!

In March, 1989, a solar flare caused the largest geomagnetic storm in 30 years, knocking out a power grid in Quebec for nine hours. Part of the power grid in the northeastern United States also experienced disruptions. Geomagnetic storms were blamed for failure of a weather satellite in 1994 and of a telephone communication satellite in January, 1997. Sunspots have been increasing toward an expected peak in the year 2000 with events as large as those in 1989 expected.

Source: Reported by Randolph Schmid, Second solar flare of week reported, Associated Press 11/7/97

outages. But there could be localized blackouts. Power companies plan for this possibility. Typical contingency plans include the purchase of power from other sources, often neighboring power companies. If the company cannot purchase enough power from other sources, part of the plan may include the sharing of available power production, resulting in the sharing of power outages within the company's service area. This would mean the rotation of power shutdowns among the various areas served by a specific power company.

Power Generation and Consumption

As noted, January 1, 2000 is likely to be a cold period for many parts of the United States. It is important, therefore, to look at year-2000 risks in the generation of power. Electricity is derived from several sources, the most prominent being nuclear, fossil fuel, natural gas, and hydroelectric. In many respects, risks to the major sources of power as a result of the year-2000 problem boil down to regulatory control and availability. Some sources are more susceptible to one form of disruption than another.

Nuclear Power Generation: Power generated from nuclear power plants accounts for approximately 20% of all the power generated in the United States. In some areas, nuclear power provides as much as 40% of the power supply[4] and even more in some individual states, especially in the northeast which is the region that relies most on nuclear power in the United States.

The Nuclear Regulatory Commission (NRC) in September, 1997 prepared a document regarding the year 2000[5] which included the following statement:[6]

Although the staff believes that safety-related safe shutdown systems will function as intended, nevertheless, in the worst case, the staff can hypothesize a scenario involving a potential common-mode failure to several non-safety-related, but important, computer- based systems necessary for plant operation that could significantly challenge the plant staff, e.g., a licensee could be faced with a plant trip as a result of a Year 2000 problem which results in the loss of offsite power and subsequent complications in tracking post-shutdown plant status and recovery due to a loss of emergency data collection and communications systems. Note that even under such a scenario, plant operators are trained to use their symptom-based emergency procedures and safety-post accident monitoring parameter indications to maintain safe plant shutdown conditions.

The consequence of this scenario is the possible shutdown of the plant, resulting in the loss of power generation. Any nuclear plant shutdown would be investigated by the NRC. Thus, plants which are forced to shutdown due to year-2000 problems may be offline for an unknown period of time—not only for repairs, but also for completion of a government investigation. Government regulatory control, therefore, is one of the potential risks to nuclear power production as a result of the year-2000 problem.

Coal: Coal is the primary supply of electrical power for the vast majority of the country. In 1996, coal supplied up to 57% of the nation's overall electrical power. In some regions of the country, coal supplies upwards of 76% of the total fuel needs for electricity production.

Coal, like natural gas, can be stored and reserves can be built up. However, unlike other power sources, such as hydroelectric and nuclear, coal needs to be delivered, primarily by railroad. There are year-2000 concerns with delivery systems, a topic explored in greater detail in another chapter. Common sense dictates that if there are problems with the delivery of coal, there may be power shortages.

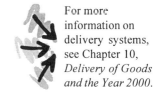 For more information on delivery systems, see Chapter 10, *Delivery of Goods and the Year 2000.*

Hydroelectric: Hydroelectric sources play a smaller role overall as a fuel source in the production of electricity in the United States, about 11%. Like other fuel sources, however, there are large regional differences. The northwest is the area of the country most dependent on hydroelectric sources. The vast potential of rivers, like the Columbia, has made the northwest the envy of the country as those living there have among the lowest electricity bills in the nation.

Fortunately, year-2000 risks involved in the production of hydroelectric power do not appear to be very great because there are less inherent risks involved. Hydroelectric sources of power are not as heavily regulated as other fuel sources and the delivery of fuel, water in this case, is also not of concern.

Natural Gas: Natural gas is a fossil fuel, formed from ancient organic matter located in the earth's crust. Natural gas provides approximately 9% of the fuel used in the overall production of electricity in the United States, the fourth highest source behind coal, nuclear, and hydroelectric sources. In some areas of the country, natural gas provides up to 34% of the overall fuel supply used for the generation of electricity.

Natural gas is obtained from very deep wells, some as deep as 30,000 feet. It is collected and moved through gathering lines to processing plants where impurities are removed. The gas is then sent via more pipelines to utility systems where it is stored or sent to a local gas utility. Pumps are located every 50 or 60 miles along the pipeline to create pressure in order to push the gas along.[7]

Natural gas can also be stored. There are huge, underground natural gas storage facilities throughout the United States, with the largest reserves in Michigan, Texas, Pennsylvania, and Illinois. As of 1995, over three *trillion* cubic feet of natural gas had been stored nationwide.[8]

Ease of transportation is another advantage. Most natural gas is delivered via a network of pipes with only a small percentage being delivered by truck. Therefore, unlike coal, fewer potential sources of disruption exist to create year-2000 problems.

However, there are some potential year-2000 concerns about the continued availability of natural gas. First, much of the delivery system is reliant on electric pumps to push the gas through pipelines. While some of these pumps have independent sources of power, others are tied into the electric grid. Second, natural gas must go through a process to remove impurities. The computerized regulation and measurement of these processes represent an area of year-2000 risk that could delay or reduce the availability of natural gas.

The Electric Power Grid

After electricity has been produced from the various fuel sources, it must be transported. The power needed for our coffee grinders to grind or our refrigerators to cool is directed through a system commonly referred to as *the electric grid*. The electric grid is similar to a giant highway system through which electricity is delivered to individuals, families, businesses, and government agencies.

This power highway is huge. In the United States, it is currently comprised of over 6,000 generating units, almost 500,000 miles of bulk transmission lines, approximately 12,000 major substations, and countless lower-voltage distribution transformers controlled by more than 100 separate control centers whose job it is to coordinate joint responsibility for its smooth operation.[9]

Given such a vast network with so many interdependent parts, what is the likelihood there are year-2000 date dependencies built into the system? Some contend it is unlikely that the electrical grid will have year-2000 problems. However, others strongly believe that there will be power supply problems, especially since these systems use embedded chip technologies.

> One electric power plant alone may have thousands of embedded systems. Without testing, the potential impact of Year 2000 errors could cause some embedded systems to malfunction, possibly resulting in a ripple effect across a portion of the grid. Because of the interconnected nature of the grid, it is important to test for malfunctions in interconnected systems as much as is feasible.[10]

Because it is generally difficult to assess embedded-system weakness, any year-2000 impact is not well understood. But due to the interconnected

Time Out!

Trouble from outer space—geomagnetic storms are another potential problem for the electrical grid. The earth's magnetic field captures particles carried by the solar wind. These particles flow through the electric grid causing differences in voltages between ground points. Much of the grid is located in northern latitudes, near the north magnetic pole and in regions of igneous rock which is highly resistive to electrical activity. This high resistance encourages geomagnetically-induced currents to flow in the power transmission lines situated above the rock resulting in potentially higher frequencies of blackouts.

Source: John Kappenman, Lawrence Zanetti, and William Radasky, Earth in Space, Vol. 9, No. 7, March 1997, Geomagnetic Storms Can Threaten Electric Power Grid, pp. 9-11, American Geophysical Union.

nature of the power industry and the widespread use of embedded-chip technologies, there is cause for concern.

Billing

We might expect to be most affected by the failure to receive electricity or gas, but one of the most unexpected impacts of year-2000 failure in the power industry may strike at our pocketbooks. Wildly inaccurate bills can be the result of lack of year-2000 compliance. And what if we refuse to pay? Could our power be shut off?

In the power industry, billing systems are considered mission critical. Therefore, the computers that handle billing are of top priority to most power companies, as with any business. However, while you may get a *nonsense bill* (an inaccurate bill caused by year-2000 date problems), the good news is power companies can't shut off your power without going through a series of steps, including contacting you or making several documented attempts to reach you, depending on the laws in your area. A power company may not realize a nonsense bill has been sent out and relies on customers to report such occurrences.

The Last Word—Light at the End of the Tunnel?

Ours is a power-hungry society. We are dependent upon the stable production and delivery of electricity to fuel our daily lives. Diligent year-2000 preparation is necessary to assure the flow of electricity will continue. Unfortunately, the current status of the industry is not well understood, as noted in recent

Time Out!

In addition to the cycles of the moon around the earth and earth around the sun, the sun has a repeating pattern called the solar cycle. The solar cycle is a recurrent period of magnetic activity that corresponds to an increase in sunspot activity and solar flares. These magnetic phenomena cause difficulties on the earth as they interfere with radio, television, telecommunications activity, and can cause wide-spread blackouts. After 22 years, the solar cycle completes and begins anew. The 22nd year of the current solar cycle ends, as you may have guessed, in the year 2000.

Source: 1997 Grolier Multimedia Encyclopedia, V9.0.1, Grolier Interactive Inc testimony before the House or Representatives: "the extent of complete Year 2000 work within the energy industry is largely unknown. Compilation of this information has been inadequate."[11]

Water

Scoping the Problem—Water, Water Everywhere . . .

Like electrical power, we tend to assume water will be available when we need it. When we turn on the tap, we expect water to pour out. And do we use a lot of water! In the United States in 1995, we used *26.1 billion gallons per day* for domestic (e.g., household) uses.[12] In addition to household uses, we use water for many other purposes, including raising livestock, irrigation of the crops that feed the nation, cooling of thermoelectric power plants, mining, and a myriad of other industrial and commercial reasons. For all purposes, as a nation we used about *341 billion gallons* of water *per day* in 1995.[13]

Water is not only critical for our basic human needs, but also for the health of our economy, so much so, that the National Public Water System Supervision Program proclaimed "the future health and economic welfare of the Nation's population are dependent upon a continuing supply of fresh uncontaminated water."[14] But, we've already seen that year-2000 problems can place the necessities of daily life in jeopardy. The question explored in this section is how year-2000 problems can impact our water supply.

Source

The water we use comes from surface and ground sources, such as rivers, lakes, and deep underground wells. Some cities located along the California coast, such as Santa Barbara, have desalinization plants as a third source. This is rather rare, however.

The advantage of obtaining water from rivers and lakes is that gravity plays a role in getting the water to the user. The idea of using gravity to move water along its way is not new—the Romans used gravity to deliver water via aquaducts. If the water source is higher than the end location, the downward pull of gravity is all that is needed to deliver water. Today, gravity

Time Out!

Water, water everywhere? While water makes up roughly 75% of the earth's surface, as a percentage not much is readily available for human consumption. Here is the make-up of water on the planet:

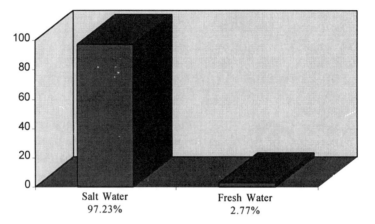

Source: <www.ce.vt.edu/enciro2/wtprimer/desalt/desalt.html>

serves as the primary means of water pressure and delivery for cities near mountains.

But not all areas of the country can receive their water from higher sources because there are no mountainous areas nearby. So alternate means of supplying pressure must be used in place of gravity to push water along. In some parts of the country, pumps bring water to the surface from deep underground wells, push it on to the treatment plant, and finally on to meet the needs of the population. Many of these pumps have their own dedicated power supply. However, in some instances, these pumps are powered by the same electrical supply as residences and businesses. This means that water supplies may be at risk if the power supply goes off line.

Storage and Distribution

The distribution of water in a city is not unlike the network of power lines that constitute the power grid for the country—only on a smaller scale. Still, even in a moderate-sized city, there are hundreds or even thousands of miles of underground pipe. In Seattle, water is currently distributed via a network of 1,828 miles of pipe. In Los Angeles, this number increases to over 7,100 miles.

Just how is water pushed through all these pipes? Generally, pumps or gravity supply the force. You've probably noticed large water storage units placed high on towers or on hills. This placement lets gravity supply the pressure needed to get the water to its destination.

Increasingly, the flow of water through this network of pipes is managed by a series of automated processes, sometimes referred to as *smart valves*. These valves use embedded technology, and as with most embedded technology, it's unclear just what might happen with these valves in the year 2000. In addition to these smart valves, computers may also be used to open and control valves across the pipeline network.

Some problems have already been discovered with water supplies. In 1997, officials in a midwestern town discovered that software controlling the valves in the water system was not year-2000 compliant, and, as such, would not work after the year 2000 without repair.[15] Obviously, if there are mass malfunctions of such technology, the risks to the availability and safety of the water supply could be disastrous. In addition, the malfunction of such technology could potentially lead to the premature release of untreated water or waste water, resulting in environmental damage and health problems.

Water Quality and Testing

Water quality is important to all of us. It's common to see or hear of reports about water being contaminated by various pollutants or bacteria. In the United States, the quality of water is regulated by the federal government through the Public Water System Supervision Program under the U.S. Environmental Protection Agency (EPA). The federal government currently regulates 81 individual contaminants, including lead, Giardia, and even radioactive substances.[16] High contaminant levels, inadequate treatment techniques, and failure to adequately monitor and report can result in violations of these government regulations. In 1996, 26% of community water supply systems reported one or more violations.[17] Obviously, the safety of our water supply is a serious concern.

Monitoring water quality is an ongoing and continuous process, both before treatment and after. Water quality is measured either in labs that obtain water samples manually, called *grab samples*, or online by a computer. The testing of water is a fairly complex process and varies depending on where the water is acquired, either ground or surface, the specific contaminant being measured, and whether the measure is before or after treatment has taken place.

Equipment used for such testing can be highly sophisticated and may be at risk for having year-2000 problems. In addition, test data and other important information is stored and analyzed on computer systems that may or may not be year-2000 compliant.

The Last Word—But Not a Drop to Drink?

A safe, readily available water supply is critical for the health of our society, the economy, and for basic human survival. The year-2000 problem places the safe supply of water that we have come to take for granted at risk by challenging the invisible infrastructure that delivers it to our homes and businesses. With thousands of water utilities around the country, each responsible for assessing and evaluating year-2000 compliance, the task of assuring water quality and safety is both daunting and vital. While we must rely on the experts in these fields to take care of the bigger issues, we can reduce personal risk through education and responsible actions.

Timely Tips—Guidelines for the Millennium

Just how dependent are we on power and water? Take a quick mental inventory. Most of us find ourselves using electricity from the moment we wake to turn off the alarm on our electric clocks. Soon after, we're turning on the lights, perhaps using an electric toothbrush, drinking a cup of coffee made by an automatic coffee maker, enjoying a hot shower, drying our hair with a blow dryer, listening to the morning news on the radio while we take waffles from the freezer and pop them into the toaster, fry bacon and eggs on the stove—and we haven't even stepped out the door yet!

If you really want to have a *no-surprises* understanding of the power dependencies in your home, you may want to conduct a power and water assessment:

Assessing vulnerability: To begin the assessment process for power and water, you may want to do a 24-hour item-by-item list. Write down each use of power and water as you move through the day. Be sure to do this for both a weekday and a weekend day as your routine will be different. You may also want to log uses of power and water for automatic functions such as heating, sprinkler, and security systems. If a member of your family uses medical equipment that requires power or water, note that as well. When you complete this part of the assessment, you will have a list of where you are vulnerable to year-2000 power and water outages.

Assessing comfort level: After assessing your power and water needs, you will want to consider the comfort level that is important to you and your family. If you are comfortable roughing it, as you would on a camping trip, then how you address your water and power needs will be different than if you *must* have your television and electric blanket.

Assessing duration: Equally important is estimating how long you may need to deal with outages. There are no firm guidelines for this, but people who live where January 2000 will be cold will probably want to take a more conservative approach and err on the side of safety.

POWER

Use the following questions as a guide to educate yourself about your power source and to help identify areas of risk.
- What is the source of production of electricity in your area?
- What are the backup or contingency plans in your area should there be a power outage or shortage?

Refer to Appendix A for information on the primary sources of electricity production on a state-by-state basis.

Alternate Power Source

Depending on the level of security you want, you may choose to buy a power generator for backup heat, light, and refrigeration needs. Although this may not be practical for some due to cost or space considerations, home owners may want to consider this option. Remember to take into consideration the need to store fuel for your generator. Also keep in mind that a generator is likely to be one of those items that will increase in price as we get closer to the year 2000 due to growing demand.

Heating your home

- If you heat your home with some sort of storable fuel such as propane, heating oil, or wood, you will probably want to lay in extra supplies well before the winter of 1999. Consider renting or leasing extra fuel tanks.
- Those who use public utilities, such as natural gas or electricity, will want a backup source of heat. If you have been considering installing a wood-burning stove or fireplace, now may be the time to do so. Stoves are superior for heating purposes, but fireplaces can be made more efficient by use of a convection air system. Be sure to check local regulations; some urban areas limit wood burning. You will also want to be sure you have matches or lighters if needed.
- Space heaters powered by kerosene, white gas, or propane are options. Larger versions are available from department stores while smaller heaters can be found where camp equipment is sold. Remember, this choice will require a safe storage area for extra fuel. Be sure that your equipment is appropriate for indoor use.
- If you live in a sunny part of the country, you may want to consider a passive solar heating system. While requiring a considerable financial investment, solar heat is an elegant solution for many reasons, not the least of which is a cleaner environment.

The Ultimate Space Heater: If none of these options appeal to you, consider spending the winter months of 2000 in a warmer climate. Plan ahead to visit family members who live in the southern parts of the country or rent a house or apartment temporarily. Heading south for the winter may be a good alternative for anyone who has health concerns or physical limitations that would make it difficult to manage unpredictable heating problems.

Alternate Light Sources

As winter nights are long, people often must get up before dawn. Candlelight may be romantic, but after a couple of hours, you will probably want a brighter source of light. Camping stores are excellent sources for alternative lighting. Many options are available, from the old standby Coleman lantern to battery powered lamps. Once again, remember to stock additional fuel or batteries as necessary. You may want to try some of the new light sticks that glow brightly enough to read by. These lights work through a safe chemical means and don't need electricity.

Cooking Alternatives

Hot meals are essential in winter. Consider these alternatives as you make your plans.
- Wood-burning stoves or fireplaces can double for cooking. If you are having a fireplace installed, consider attaching a swivel hook to the side from which to hang a pot.
- The barbecue grill in your backyard can serve as a temporary cooking source. Although this may seem like an adequate alternative at first, cooking outside in really cold weather can rapidly lose its appeal.
- Camping stores are some of the best sources for portable stoves. You can find everything from tiny, one-burner stoves that will almost fit into a pocket to large stoves with as many burners as a conventional stove. Again, make sure your choice is safe for indoor use unless you plan to cook on the patio or in your backyard. Remember to buy fuel.

Refrigeration Tips

If the electricity goes out for any length of time, food stored in the refrigerator and freezer is in jeopardy. Consider the following:
- Eat what is in the refrigerator first; save dry or canned food supplies for later.
- Keep the freezer closed until you are ready to use the food.
- Never refreeze food which has thawed . If you have more food than you can eat before it spoils, have a party and invite the neighbors.
- Never eat food that is questionable; food poisoning can be serious as well as painful.

Tips for Coping with Power Surges
- Power surges can damage anything that is plugged in. And many appliances and other equipment, such as computers, can be very expensive to replace—not to mention the problem of losing access to important data files on your computer. If you suspect that your power supply may be erratic, the simplest solution is to unplug electrical appliances and equipment when not in use.
- In the case of a blackout, the stress of bringing power back on line to the electrical generating system is huge. When all the devices that were left

on are powered up simultaneously, the demand load can be 600% of normal–a great source of stress on the generating equipment and the power grid as a whole.[18] To reduce stress to the power grid, only use essential appliances and equipment.

- Be cautious in relying on inexpensive surge protectors; they may not provide the surge control you want and, therefore, may not always prevent damage. In addition, surge protectors don't allow you to save data and shut down your computer if power goes out.
- People who spend many hours on a home computer may want to invest in a more serious level of protection, such as a backup or uninterrupted power supply (UPS), which also provides surge protection. These devices help regulate the power to your system by stepping up low power and reducing high-power surges. And because these devices also provide power if power should go out, you have time to safely shut down your applications and system, protecting your investment. These devices can be found in computer stores and catalogs, and range from $60 to $500 depending on the options.

Alternate Information and Entertainment Sources

When the power goes out, it is easy to feel isolated. Consider how you will keep in touch with the outside world and keep occupied.

- You may want to have a battery-powered radio to keep in touch with what is happening in the outside world.
- Battery-powered televisions are also available, but tend to have a relatively short battery life. If you go for this option, you may want to reserve their use for news programs and updates.
- Our children have grown up in a wired world. If the television and Nintendo are out of commission, you may want to have books, board games, coloring books and craft projects available to keep the them, and adults, occupied.

Other Power Considerations

- If you live in a high-rise building and suffer a power loss, your elevators may stop working. Unless you are particularly athletic, getting up and down numerous flights of stairs may be difficult. Carrying groceries or children will make it even tougher. And elderly people will need assistance.

Making arrangements in advance to stay with family or friends in the event of a power outage may be a good idea.
- Of course, you should stock up on warm clothing including hats, mittens, and long underwear. Don't forget that children, especially early teens, grow rapidly and may need larger sizes. Blankets, comforters, or sleeping bags are a must in colder climates.

WATER

Gathering information about the water utility in your area will also be important; contacting your utility company directly is the best way. Here are some questions to help get you started:
- Where does your water come from? Well, ground sources, or a combination?
- Do the pumping stations have a dedicated power source, or are they tied directly to the power grid?
- What backup systems or contingency plans are in place to deal with emergencies?

Caution: Don't assume all utilities are the same. It's important to evaluate your own water supply to determine your year-2000 risk. The Environmental Protection Agency (EPA) reports that there were 172,248 water systems in the United States and its territories in 1996. Some wells have dedicated or separate power supplies. Most water utilities try to store enough water to last for several days or even up to weeks. Water utilities will often have backup sources of power to keep their equipment working. In addition, they probably have emergency plans to supply drinking water if their system fails. For example, shipping water into an area has been done when the regular water supply was unusable or unavailable because of a natural disaster, such as an earthquake. Be sure to find out what plans your utility company has.

Water Storage Tips

Plan for a minimum of one gallon of water per day for each person in your household. If you do hard labor or exercise and perspire heavily, allow for more. Nursing mothers will also want to do the same. Multiply this figure by the number of days supply you wish to have. You will also need water for cooking and washing. And don't forget your pets' water needs.

If you choose to store water to last for a period of time, use the following as a guide:

- Bottled water can be purchased from local distributors. Look for glass or hard, clear plastic bottles. The shelf life of bottled water is limited, so be aware of dates on bottles or mark your bottles with dates. If you routinely use bottled water, consider buying an extra bottle each time you shop.
- Some people may want to fill their own bottles with tap water. If you choose this alternative, be aware that the shelf life of tap water is considerably less than commercially bottled water. Thus, you will want to add a purifier to your water, such as a few drops of plain household bleach. Read the instructions on the bleach bottle for the correct amounts.
- If you live in a cold climate, be sure you store your water where it won't freeze and crack the container.

Hidden Sources of Water

The Red Cross lists the following sources of water on its web site (www.redcross.org).

Inside Your House:
- Water in your hot-water tank
- Water pipes in your house
- Ice cubes
- Water in the reservoir of your toilet tank (not the bowl)

Outside Sources of Water:
- Rainwater
- Streams, rivers, and other moving bodies of water
- Ponds and lakes
- Natural springs

If you use water from any of the above outside sources, you will want to be sure the water is safe. Many camping stores offer a variety of filtering devices which purify water. Be sure that the device you pick doesn't just alter the taste. You need one that gets rid of the microorganisms that can be harmful. Other options include adding iodine tablets and boiling water for a sufficient amount of time to kill microorganisms.

Waste Products

If you aren't getting water, your toilet isn't either. Chemical toilets provide a short-term solution. Make certain to purchase adequate supplies of the necessary chemical additives if you choose this option.

Waste products can be stored temporarily in heavy duty plastic bags which tie securely at the top. You will want to keep filled bags away from other stored items and where they will not be inadvertently punctured. Never dispose of waste products where they can contaminate food or water sources or pose a hazard to other people.

Billing Problems with Power and Water Services

Most records at power companies are backed up in the event something happens to computer systems. While it's not likely that your records would be lost, as a safeguard keep a copy of your records and payments.

Good records won't prevent you from receiving an incorrect bill. However, while you may get a *nonsense bill* if the company doesn't fix its computer systems, the good news is power and water utilities can't shut off your power automatically. The utility must go through a series of steps before shutting off power or water to a home or business. Steps typically include making direct contact with you or showing several documented attempts were made to contact you. The latter could take the form of registered mail. However, the steps that your utility must take is dependent on the laws in your area.

The power or water utility may not know you have received a nonsense bill. *You* are responsible for taking the action necessary to insure that your bill is accurate and your account is up to date.

Test Run

There is no better way to assess your year-2000 readiness than living a day without the availability of power and water. At the end of twenty-four hours, you should have a clearer picture of your level of preparedness. Make any adjustments and additions needed. Then relax and pat yourself on the back for a job well done.

[1] Fisher, Frank. January 9, 1998. Ice storm, floods: 16 dead over wide area. *Seattle Times*.

[2] Press Release by Senator Bennett and the Senate Committee on the Year 2000, Y2K Committee Announces Survey Results Measuring Y2K Preparedness of Nation's Largest Utilities, June 12, 1998. Available at <http://www.senate.gov/~y2k/news/pr061298.html>

[3] *Ibid.*

[4] Table 23, Sources of Energy for Electric Generation by State and Energy Source, 1996 Statistical Yearbook, Edison Electric Institute.

U.S. Nuclear Regulatory Commission, SECY-97-213, September 24, 1997. Available at
[5] <http://www.nrc/gov/NRC/Y2K/S97213.html>

[6] U.S. Nuclear Regulatory Commission, appendix B of SECY-97-213, Year 2000 and Operating Nuclear Power Plants: Scope of the Year 2000 Problem at Operating Nuclear Power Plants, September 24, 1997. Available at <http://www.nrc/gov/NRC/Y2K/S97213B.html>

[7] Gas Industry Online. < http://www.aga.com>

[8] The Value of Underground Storage in Today's Natural Gas Market, DOE/EIA-0591(95). Available from the Energy Information Administration web site at <http://www.eia.doe.gov>

[9] Kappenman, John, Zanetti, Lawrence, and Radasky, William. March 1997. Geomagnetic storms can threaten electric power grid. *Earth in Space*, Vol. 9, No. 7., pp. 9-11. American Geophysical Union.

[10] Hirning, Kathleen. Testimony before the Subcommittee on Technology, Committee of Science, United States House of Representatives, May 14, 1998. Available at <http://www.house.gov/science/hirning_05-14.htm>

[11] *Ibid.*

[12] Water Q&A, United States Geological Survey. Available at <http://wwwga.usgs.gov/edu/qahome.html>

[13] *Ibid.*.

[14] FY 1996 National Compliance Report. The National Drinking Water Program: An Overview. The National Public Water System Supervision Program. Information on drinking water is available at the EPA's Office of Ground Water and Drinking Water. <http://www.epa.gov/ogwdw>

[15] Kim, James. April 29, 1997. One-man army fights his city's Year 2000 hitch. *USA Today*, Money section.

[16] FY 1996 National Compliance Report. The National Drinking Water Program: An Overview. The National Public Water System Supervision Program. Information on drinking water is available at the EPA's Office of Ground Water and Drinking Water. <http://www.epa.gov/ogwdw>

[17] *Ibid.*

[18] Kappenman, John, Zanetti, Lawrence, and Radasky, William. March, 1997. Geomagnetic Storms Can Threaten Electric Power Grid. Earth in Space, Vol. 9, No. 7. pp. 9-11. American Geophysical Union.

Chapter 3

Food and the Year 2000

In this chapter you will learn:

- How the food industry in this country has changed
- Why farming and satellites need each other
- What factors could lead to food shortages
- How food quality could be impacted by the year-2000 problem

The Staff of Life

In times of crisis, food is one of the first commodities to disappear off store shelves. In countries with unstable governments, as witnessed recently in Russia, people stockpile foods to prepare for periods of instability and potential civil unrest. In the United States, people usually stockpile food supplies in preparation for natural disasters, such as hurricanes, floods and tornadoes. The reason for stocking food at all is, of course, simple—people need food to survive in an uncertain future.

Fortunately, we have enjoyed an ample supply of food in the United States and generally have not suffered widespread shortages. Nor have we been subject to the long lines and barren shelves seen on television in countries undergoing crises. However, the year-2000 problem is proving to be as much a concern as any flood or tornado for some. On the increase are stories of individuals spending tens of thousands of dollars for a several year supply of freeze-dried foods and other goods.[1] Is this over reacting? Should everyone be stockpiling basic foodstuffs for survival? How complicated is the problem and how does one make a rational decision?

Scoping the problem—From Farm to Fork

In the not too distant past, there was a relatively short distance between the food grown on farms to the food on our tables. Many families, in fact, grew much of their own food in small gardens. Today, however, there are many middlemen between the food source and our pantry. Many companies are involved in food processing, and government agencies are involved in the inspection of foods.

Farmers, ranchers, processors, inspectors, distributors, grocery stores, restaurants, delis, all the people involved in the production of food, have created a more complex *food chain* than previously existed. Any break in this food chain has the potential for leading to food shortages. An important change from the recent past is the reliance on computerized, automated processes in everything from farming to the delivery of the final food product.

It is important to have an understanding of the food chain—from farm to fork—in order to assess your needs and develop a strategy for dealing with the year-2000 problem.

Farming

Farming and ranching increasingly are accepting and benefiting from the use of computers and other technologies. Many jobs, as varied as irrigation and milking, are automated and controlled in whole or part by computers. For example, databases that keep records of the milk production of individual cows have been used for years. Personal computers are not uncommon and are considered by some as integral to farm operations as any other piece of equipment.

Farming is undergoing a transformation—some call it a revolution—that calls for the use of everything from sophisticated computer databases storing vast amounts of crop and weather information to global positioning systems (GPS) for mapping farmers' fields. Information gleaned from this technology allows farmers to analyze soil type, fertility levels, insect infestation, yield and weather history, productivity potential, and water needs—all in order to increase crop yields. The advantage of this *precision farming* is that it helps maximize crop yield and keeps the price of food low—all through automation and efficiency. The greatest disadvantage, of course, is that the food industry, and we, are increasingly dependent on this technology.

For more information on global positioning systems, see Chapter 10, *Delivery of Goods and the Year 2000.*

We know that precision farming instruments, specifically receivers making use of global positioning satellites, may be susceptible to either the year-2000 problem or the end-of-week (EOW) rollover problem. Similar to the year-2000 problem, the EOW rollover problem has to do with how the Global Positioning System (GPS) counts time. The GPS will rollover on August 21,

Time Out!

Grains make up 80% of the world's food consumption. A nutritious mix of carbohydrates, proteins, and vitamins, grains are easy to transport and store. The green revolution of the last thirty years has increased per acre yield dramatically and changed what crops are grown. Wheat, rice and corn are now the three major crops worldwide. A full forty percent of the world's grain harvest is fed to livestock. It takes eight pounds of grain to produce one pound of beef and two pounds of grain to produce one pound of chicken. And in the last fifty years, people have increased the amount of meat they eat fourfold.

Source: National Geographic, The National Geographic Society, Washington, DC, October, 1998. p 65.

1999, and equipment not compliant with either the year-2000 problem or EOW may be affected.

Since precision farming is a relatively new concept, it is not clear how much year-2000 failures in this area could impact food production. Obviously, the loss of this technology wouldn't stop cows from producing milk or crops from growing. However, some, especially large corporations, may be forced to return to more traditional methods of farming and ranching. The loss of efficiencies gained through the use of valuable information and automation could have implications for the productivity, cost, and, potentially, the availability of food.

But there are other aspects critical to farming that don't involve precision farming technologies. Farmers need seeds and fertilizer for growing crops as well as feed for livestock. The year-2000 readiness of the feed and fertilizer industries is outside the control of farmers. These companies face the same year-2000 problems as everybody else and must make sure their computer systems, including their embedded systems, are year-2000 compliant. Of course, these industries depend on other sectors for receiving power, water, and the delivery of supplies. Farming, ranching, feed and fertilizer industries are all integral and interdependent links in the food chain. A year-2000 weakness in any link threatens the whole chain.

Food Processors Plants

As a society we have become ever more reliant on the ready-to-eat or near-ready-to-eat foods we purchase in restaurants and grocery stores . For working

Time Out!

Your nose or your French fries? Have a craving from French fries? Thank the Inca Indians of Peru. Potatoes were first cultivated in Peru about 200 BC, although they look considerably different than those today. The first potatoes ranged in size from as small as a nut to as large as an apple, and the colors varied from red and gold to blue and black. In the 16th century, Spanish conquistadors in the new World discovered potatoes and took them back to Europe along with gold. Because the potato is a member of the nightshade family, some considered it to be poisonous or evil. It took drastic measures for the potato to be accepted. Germany's King Frederick William ordered peasants to plant and eat potatoes or have their noses sliced off!

Source: <www.idbsu.edu/bsuradio/potato/ancient.htm>

parents with families, single parents, and other hardworking individuals, the convenience of these processed foods affords us a bit more of another precious commodity—time. How often, for example, do you go or take the children to McDonalds?

Food processing companies are candidates for year-2000 problems. These processing plants can be very sophisticated, depending for their success on efficient, clock-like operations. As such, everything from assembly lines to refrigeration units must be checked in order to determine their year-2000 compliance. A stoppage of the production lines of these food giants could very well impact the availability of some of processed foods we have grown accustomed to enjoying. When talking about processed foods, the first items you probably think about are foods such as spaghetti sauce, frozen pizza, and TV dinners. However, processed foods include a much broader group of foodstuffs. That jar of peanut butter, can of tuna, and box of cereal in your pantry, as well as the bag of frozen green beans and concentrated orange juice in your freezer, are all processed food items. And let's not forget the bottle of oil you use for cooking. This list doesn't even scratch the surface—there are hundreds more processed foods that we simply don't think of as being processed foods.

Grocery Stores

Whether you know it or not, you probably practice just-in-time inventory management in your pantry—buying only what you need for a given period of time, one week, maybe two. Very few people buy food in sufficient quantities to last them for several months or even a year. This kind of management reduces waste because fewer products go bad, and it allows you to use your money for other purposes.

Grocery stores, of course, must also manage their inventory, but on a much grander scale. Large inventories of products require a tremendous amount of capital. Sometimes these products don't sell right away, tying up the money that could have been used elsewhere. Stores try hard to avoid having too much of a product that isn't selling, while not having enough of the products that are in demand. Thus, grocery stores, like many businesses, may use a just-in-time method of managing their inventory. Although a simplification, this generally means knowing how much of a product sold last year during a particular time period. This information helps stores to forecast demand in the near term, thereby avoiding having too much or too little of each item.

Sometimes, however, there are problems with this type of inventory management. This process is akin to driving a car using the rear-view mirror as your guide. Because they aren't looking forward, some stores may not take into account unusual events or circumstances that impact the demand for a particular product or products. The year 2000 may be one of those unusual events that creates a problem in forecasting adequate—or the right kind of—food supplies.

Here is an example of how this problem can play out. Several year ago, a large organization selected a new location for their annual convention. The restaurants in the area prepared by stocking the goods they normally sold, hamburgers, steaks, wines, beer, and the like—the kind of food the typical convention attendee enjoys.

Time Out!

There was nothing like it. It was a very special design screw-top closure with glass threads and lip at the mouth of the jar. Perfect for canning. John Mason patented his design in 1858. Later in the century, Ball bought Mr. Mason's patent, but retained Mason's name on their jars to show the company used his famous design. In the 1930's, Ball would add grippers, raised vertical lines on the sides of the jar to allow a firmer grip when opening. Generations of men and women remember the Mason Jar and associate it with canning the fruits and vegetables from their home gardens at the end of a long, hot summer. The Ball company no longer makes glass containers, having sold that part of their business in 1996.

Source: <www.ball.com/bhome/gblaq.html#home>

By the end of the first day, it was obvious something was very wrong. None of the attendees were eating at the restaurants. Had the restaurant managers known that the convention group was made up of several thousand vegetarians, who also did not drink alcoholic beverages, they may have altered their menu a bit and had more business. Predicting future need by looking in the rear-view mirror prevented these restaurateurs from seeing what was coming. Reportedly the following year, the restaurant managers got it right—salad bars stretched as far as the eye could see!

In addition to a potential lack of foresight and planning, there is another issue that could cause grocery store and food businesses problems—dependence on the rest of the food chain. Keeping just enough food products as can be sold in the near future makes stores susceptible to the production, inventory, and delivery problems that the food processing plants, distributors, farmers, and so on could have. And because stores typically don't stock more than what they need until the next shipment, they could find themselves without *any* product to sell.

The result of either scenario? Shortages.

Delivery Systems

The practice of just-in-time inventory management in stores, of course, also makes timely delivery all that much more crucial. Forecasting is worthless if products don't reach the stores. Likewise, a good harvest is worthless if it sits on the dock. All the sophisticated technology used to increase crop yields can be for naught if the product isn't delivered for further processing or for sale in stores. And many of these shipments—such as fresh produce and fruit—*demand* timely delivery.

Many forms of transportation are used in the delivery of food—trucks, trains, and even cargo ships delivering products from other countries, such as fruit from South America. And, of course, delivery systems have their own year-2000 concerns, including tracking, scheduling, and routing. Interestingly, modern day shipping relies on global positioning satellites just as some aspects of precision farming do. GPS systems have their own unique concern with regards to a date-related computer problems.

Delivery systems, of course, operate up and down the food chain. Food and livestock are not only delivered *from* farms and ranches, but also critical supplies, including seeds, fertilizer, and feed, are delivered *to* farmers and ranchers. Without these supplies farmers and ranchers would find it difficult, if not impossible, to continue feeding the population.

Clearly, delivery is a critical component of the food chain, and problems with delivery have the potential for resulting in delays and shortages.

Food Quality

Could the year-2000 problem impact the quality of our food? If so, how? Inspection programs ensure public health and safety. You may recall the distressing stories of E.coli poisonings resulting in a number of people becoming severely ill and others, tragically, dying. Inspection programs for public health and safety play an important role in the food chain in the United States.

The United States Department of Agriculture (USDA) is the principal inspector of the foods we eat. And, of course, it should come as no surprise that the USDA has its own year-2000 concerns. The USDA is involved in nearly all aspects of the food chain. If it does not fix its year-2000 problems, potential problems could occur, including:[2]

- The economy being adversely affected if information critical to crop and livestock providers and investors is unreliable, late, or unavailable
- The import and export of foodstuffs being delayed, thus increasing the likelihood that the goods will not reach their intended destinations before their spoilage dates
- Food distribution to schools and others being stopped or delayed
- Public health and safety becoming at risk if equipment used in the USDA's many laboratories to detect bacteria, diseases, and unwholesome foods is not year-2000 compliant
- Payment to schools, farmers, and others in rural communities being delayed or incorrectly computed

Unfortunately, the USDA is finding it has many of the same difficulties as other government organizations, including dealing with the sheer size of the task and lack of qualified personnel with sufficient knowledge on hand to address their year-2000 problems.

The Last Word—Food for Thought

Some Americans are going to stock up on food as the year 2000 gets closer. And as there is a tendency in our society to wait until the last moment, some people are going to wait until late 1999 before starting to prepare, which could increase the likelihood of panic buying.

 Panic buying can create or exaggerate food shortages. Fear has a way of building on itself and growing. Even with abundant supplies, such unnecessary, panic-driven buying could create the perception of a larger problem, resulting in increased panic buying in yet other locations. A spot shortage in one area could spread to a larger one, and so on.

As a society we are fortunate to enjoy abundant food supplies, unequaled in any other period of history. Today, there are many middleman between the farm and our pantries. As such, for a continued abundance of food and a smooth transition into the next millennium, each link in the food chain must do their part in addressing their year-2000 problems.

The good news is that having adequate food supplies for the year-2000 event is something over which we have direct control. We can make sensible, realistic plans in advance that meet our individual needs and dietary restrictions.

Timely Tips—Guidelines for the Millennium

When families were moving west in covered wagons, months were spent preparing for the journey. Women were responsible for much of the planning and provisioning. The wise wife or mother carefully assessed the needs of her family, figuring how much and what kind of food they would take, what clothing would be needed, what household utensils would be required, and what medicines might be necessary. These choices often determined the success or failure of the family's venture. Those families whose welfare was in the hands of a skillful planner stood a better chance of arriving at their destination strong and healthy.

Planning Your *Journey*

Skillful planning can go a long ways towards helping you feel comfortable and secure about the coming millennium. Especially with food, planning and preparation for the year-2000 is within your control—if you start now. Addressing the food needs of your family is an area of great importance. You'll sleep better knowing that you are prepared for the inevitable bumps in the road as we travel into the next century. The first step is assessing your family's needs.

- Start by making a list of family members, their likes and dislikes and any special food or dietary considerations.
- Next, calculate how much food your family will need for a week's worth of meals. This may be tough if you are not accustomed to making a weekly menu plan and shopping list. A good way to gather this information is to keep track of what you use to prepare meals for a week—sort of a food diary.
- Notice which foods require refrigeration or special preparation using electrical appliances such as blenders, bread makers, and mixers. Remember, should the power in your area go off, you will want to have foods that can be stored at room temperature and that are easy to prepare.

Now that you have a good idea of your family's weekly requirements, you can calculate how much food you will want to have on hand should the food supply at the grocery store be erratic due to the year-2000 problems. One month's supply should probably be a minimum. Those who like a larger margin of safety will want to increase this amount accordingly. Many of us have been thinking for sometime that it would be wise to have a few emergency supplies on hand in case of an earthquake, flood or other natural disaster. The year-2000 event may be just the impetus we need to get moving.

Preparation Tips

Before you start stocking up, you may want to have a brainstorming session with your family about the kinds of foods to store. You also may want to do a little research on what stores well.

- The Red Cross and the Department of Agriculture are good sources of information. Check their web sites at <www.redcross.com> and <www.usda.gov>
- Many churches, such as The Church of Latter Day Saints, have a tradition of community preparedness and are generous in sharing their expertise in this area.
- Many books are available on backpacking and camping cuisine; these can give you ideas on ease of preparation.

Foods That Store Well

The following foods keep well; while not inclusive, this list will help you to start thinking about the food you need:

- wheat
- vegetable oils
- honey
- dried corn
- baking powder
- soybeans
- instant coffee, tea, and cocoa
- salt
- powdered and canned milk
- bouillon products
- dry pasta
- rice, beans, lentils, split peas, barley
- canned foods

Other Food Tips

- Include vitamins, minerals, and protein supplements to assure adequate nutrition.
- In addition to basic needs, include foods for those with dietary restrictions and medical problems, such as diabetes.
- Don't forget your pets.

Other Household Items

Don't forget other non-food items you may need:

- Soap, detergent, cleansers
- Paper napkins, towels, plates
- Plastic food and trash bags
- Toilet paper
- Personal hygiene items
- Shampoo

How to Develop a Food Stockpile

Probably the easiest way to develop a stockpile is to increase gradually the amount of basic foods you normally keep on your shelves. Buying a few extra items each week makes this financially reasonable. Of course if you can afford to make larger purchases, buying in bulk is less expensive in the long run. In any case, don't wait to get started. As the year 2000 approaches panic buyers may create temporary shortages and drive prices up.

Where to Store Food Stocks

After you have developed an understanding of your food requirements, you need to consider storage options.

- Most foods keep best in a cool, dry place. Basements are ideal; temperatures will be cool and more consistent than in other parts of the house.
- If you have no basement, consider converting a closet in your house to a pantry or set up shelves in your garage.
- If you live in a climate where winters are severe, you will want to store some items such as canned goods and liquids where they will not be damaged by freezing.
- If your storage space is extremely limited, be creative. There may be room under the bed, behind the couch or even in the trunk of your car.
- If you live in an apartment building, you and other tenants may want to talk to the manager about converting a tool storage room or other area to a year-2000 provision area.
- Church groups may want to consider setting up a storage area for members and consider bulk purchases.
- How about forming a year-2000 group on the block where you live? Group energy and expertise can go a long way towards solving problems.

Food Storage Tips

- Keep food in a dry, cool place.
- Rotate your food stocks, like grocery stores do, by using the items purchased first.
- Keep food covered at all times; airtight and bug-proof containers are best.
- Open food boxes carefully so that you can close them tightly after each use.

Test Run

Once you have assembled your stockpile of food, you may want to do a test run. For one week prepare and eat only foods from your year-2000 supplies. If a week seems too long for a trial period, a weekend will give you some basic information about what you may be missing. This trial period will quickly show you if you have done a good job in anticipating you or your family's needs. You will probably notice several places where you will want to make additions or adjustments. Did you forget the spices? Did your three-year-old refuse to eat oatmeal? Plan to acquire these new items as soon as is practical. You may be tempted to skip this test phase. But there is no better way to assess your year-2000 readiness than to conduct a trial run. Enjoy the challenge of this test—and the subsequent satisfaction of knowing that you have done a good job and are prepared for the new century.

---

[1] Campbell, Joel. September 8, 1998. Huge surge in food-storage sales blamed on Y2K. *Deseret News*. Available at <http://www.desnews.com/cit/y10k0idd.htm>

[2] Willemssen, Joel C. May 14, 1998. USDA Faces Tremendous Challenges in Ensuring That Vital Public Services Are Not Disrupted. General Accounting Office. Available at <http://www.access.gpo.gov/cgi-bin/getdoc.cgi?dbname=gao&docid=f:ai98167t.txt.pdf>

Chapter 4

Healthcare and the Year 2000

In this chapter you will learn:

- What concerns exist for medical devices
- About potential problems with health insurance
- About problems Medicare is having with year-2000 compliance
- How medications could be affected by the year-2000 problem

Prescription for Well Being

Entering the year 2000 could be hazardous to your health. One expert, an academic doctor at a London Hospital, predicted that 1,500 hospital patients in Britain could die in the first weeks of the new century because of government complacency about the dangers of year-2000 failures. It was anticipated that even a small 10% computer failure rate could have devastating effects. This same article referenced the London Ambulance Service incident in 1992 and the 20 deaths alleged to have occurred as the direct result of a software problem.[1] The healthcare industry's reliance on technology, as with any other industry, does put the system at risk. But with healthcare, there are other complications that compound these technology problems. Before we look at the key issues, remember that an ounce of prevention is worth a pound of cure. There are steps you can take to minimize any risks.

Scoping the Problem—A Tightly Woven Fabric

To understand the potential impact of the year-2000 problem on our healthcare system requires a framework for understanding the bigger picture. Like a tightly woven fabric, our healthcare system is a closely knit network of insurance companies; private and public hospitals and clinics; pharmacies,

Time Out!

Clara Burton became known as The Angel of the Battlefield for her work nursing soldiers during the Civil War. In 1870, Barton traveled to Europe as a volunteer relief worker during the Franco-Prussian War. Because she was a woman, she was not permitted to work for the International Red Cross. Ten years later, in 1881, Barton founded the American Red Cross and became its first president. In contrast to the International Red Cross which provided only battlefield relief, the American Red Cross served in both times of war and peace. Barton headed the association until 1904, personally organizing many of its relief efforts.

Source: <www.redcross.org/hec/pre9000/cbarton.html> and <http://www.incwell.com/Biographies/Barton.html>

pharmaceutical and medical equipment manufactures; physicians, nurses, emergency response personnel; and government agencies such as Medicare and the Federal Drug Administration (FDA). All of these components depend on the smooth operation of the others. Each face unique year-2000 challenges and the failure of any to address these issues imperils the function of the system as a whole.

Because we don't interact with the healthcare industry unless there is need, most of us are unaware of the immense size of the healthcare industry in the United States. In his opening statement at the July 23, 1998 Senate hearing on the healthcare industry and the year-2000 problem, Senator Bob Bennett noted that healthcare is the United State's largest industry. Generating $1.7 trillion annually—more than one-seventh of the nation's economy—the system currently includes 6,000 hospitals, 800,000 doctors, and 50,000 nursing homes.

Because of sheer size, you might expect that the healthcare industry would have begun its year-2000 efforts early on. However, in comparison to other industries tackling the year-2000 problem, the healthcare industry's progress is generally perceived as lagging behind.[2] This chapter will explore several key challenges facing the healthcare industry as we near the year 2000.

Medical Technology and Devices

Sophisticated and specialized medical technology is the tool of the medical trade. Were it not available, the healthcare industry as we know it would not exist, and certainly the level of care provided would not be as high. The role of nearly all this medical technology—at a cost in the U.S. of about 58 billion dollars annually[3]—is to provide information to medical personnel so they can make informed decisions about the care of patients. It's crucial, therefore, that this information be accurate, timely, and trustworthy.

Often, high-tech medical equipment contains *embedded* computer chips— so named because the computer chip is embedded within the structure of the device. Unlike computer software, which can be more easily changed or replaced, embedded chips have program instructions burned into the chip. Why so much concern? Many of these embedded chips may include date-dependent features. Year-2000 issues could cause devices with these chips to function incorrectly or to cease to function altogether. Such equipment is found throughout hospitals, clinics, nursing homes, even in patients themselves. These devices range from sophisticated radiation dosage instruments and x-ray machines to fire-alarm and security systems. This has led to a serious concern about patient safety:

> Consider for a minute what would occur if a monitor failed to sound an alarm when a patient's heart stopped beating. Or if a respirator delivered "unscheduled breaths" to a respirator-dependent patient. Or even if a digital display were to attribute the name of one patient to medical data from another patient. Are these scenarios hypothetical, based on conjecture? No. Software problems have caused each one of these medical devices to malfunction with potentially fatal consequences. The potential danger is present.[4]

Year-2000 progress in the area of embedded devices has been a tale of two steps forward and one step back. Ideally, device manufacturers would be able to supply information regarding the year-2000 compliance of their products. Unfortunately, some of these device manufacturers have not been forthcoming with the information. Earlier this year, FDA spokesperson Sharon Snider said:

> The agency has only received Y2K [year 2000] compliance information from about 11% of the 16,000 medical devices manufacturers worldwide. Even when vendors do respond, their responses have frequently not been helpful. The Department of Veteran's Affairs recently reported that of more than 1,600 medical

device manufacturers it has contacted in the past year, 233 manufacturers did not even reply and another 187 vendors said they were not responsible for alterations because they had merged, were purchased by another company, or were no longer in business.[5]

Unfortunately, even with information from the manufacturer, the devices will need to be verified independently—a painstaking and time-consuming process as "manufacturer's model and serial numbers may be alike, but the chips and boards inside test with different responses. Some work and some fail."[6] And, the sheer number of devices in a hospital or clinic that must be checked is enormous. A well-equipped hospital can have thousands of devices, each of which must be checked for year-2000 compliance.

Healthcare Business Practices

Like any business, healthcare providers must deal with internal and external year-2000 concerns such as billing, payments, personnel information, receipt of supplies, cash flow, and so on. Many of these procedures are computerized and are at the same degree of risk as in any other business.

People receive healthcare from a wide variety of practitioners, clinics, and hospitals—each different in their year-2000 exposure. Classifying these differences by the size of the practice and type of service offered is one way of understanding the risks involved, and to assess the risk to ourselves.

Size: The size of healthcare practices show tremendous variance—from large hospital organizations such as Veteran's Medical Centers employing thousands of individuals to the small, private practice. Few studies have focused on the role size may play in year-2000 preparedness.

Most inquires have focused on the risks of the larger hospitals, and certainly, they are the organizations most likely to have large numbers of computerized equipment and devices. However, as we have seen with other business organizations, the larger organizations are also more likely to have the financial resources and personnel available to address their year-2000 problems.

It is probably the medium-sized healthcare clinics who are at greater risk as they have a significant degree of computerization needing attention but apply a lessor degree of oversight in the year-2000 compliance of their computerized devices, including embedded chips in instruments.

Smaller-sized clinics or groups of practitioners may have fewer systems to fail, but this does not mean they will be trouble free. Although the independent practitioners are less likely to have as large a number of computerized systems and devices demanding attention, they also have fewer financial resources to apply to assessment and repair. And it is important to remember that even small medical practices almost always accept insurance, frequently file electronically, and must interface with large computer-dependent entities such as insurance companies and Medicare/Medicaid.

Type of Service: Healthcare is a broad field. More and more, people are seeking treatment from alternative or complementary providers— acupuncturists, chiropractors, psychologists, naturopaths, homeopaths, and healers. Fortunately these providers generally have fewer year-2000 risks than medical practices. However, just about every provider uses some computerized processes that could be at risk, such as record keeping, appointment scheduling, patient accounts, and/or insurance filing.

Medications

Pharmacies have the same accounting, inventory, and record-keeping problems as any business and the same year-2000 risks. Pharmacies are an important component of our healthcare system because they manage and stockpile the inventory of medications needed by millions of people. Most people are familiar with pharmacies located in larger retail stores or grocery chains—but many pharmacies are also located within hospitals and medical complexes that carry not only medications for individuals, but also supplies for physicians, surgeons, and anesthetists. And few of us think at all about the manufacturers of the medications—the pharmaceutical companies themselves.

Production: When you take an aspirin or other medication, do you wonder if the dosage is off a little? Manufacturers have gone to great lengths to ensure consistency so that you can trust the medication you are taking. The manufacturing equipment which produce medicines are sensitive and closely monitored for accuracy. The dosages in many medications are small; if inaccuracies should occur, medicine could be lethal in the case of too much, and ineffective in the case of too little.

Most manufacturers are working diligently to address year-2000 issues at all levels of the production process. However, the amount of work to be done is significant. Many devices need assessment, including lab and manufacturing hardware and software, that could potentially force a shutdown or impact production of medicines if year-2000 problem are not addressed.

Time Out!

Few of us would want to face an operation or removal of a tooth without the benefit of anesthesia. But that was standard practice 150 years ago until Horace Wells, a dentist from Connecticut, developed a technique for removing teeth painlessly using nitrous oxide. In January 1845, he attempted to demonstrate his method to a group of Harvard Medical School students. But Wells misjudged the dosage and the patient screamed in pain. The students began to yell "humbug" and laughed Wells out of Boston. It wasn't until twenty-three years later that the American Dental Association and the American Medical Association acknowledged Wells' discovery.

Source: <neurosurgery.mgh.harvard.edu/History/ether3.htm>

Inventory: There are year-2000 concerns with medication inventories as well. As with many businesses, pharmacies and hospitals also practice just-in-time management of their inventory. The intention is good—to keep expenses down by stocking only what will be needed. However, if some manufacturers or distributors have year-2000 problems, pharmacies may not have sufficient amounts of needed medicines on hand.

This is not a problem if the same or similar medication is available from other companies. For example, there are a number of vendors that produce and distribute common drugs, such as aspirin. But there is greater risk if only one manufacturer produces a patented medication for which there are no alternatives. If you are taking an *uncommon* medication, prior to the year 2000 you should check with your doctor to identify your options, including alternative types or sources of medications.

Insurance/Medicare

Insurance is as integral to healthcare as are doctors and x-rays. Many individuals rely on insurance to pay for the healthcare they receive—from prescriptions to surgery. Hospitals and clinics rely on the insurance industry for the timely payment for services provided to patients. The good news is that many insurance companies have been working on their year-2000 problem for years. As a result, large, private health insurance companies are among the better prepared for the millennium. However, there is some concern that smaller and mid-size companies might find themselves at risk because they have neither the awareness of the problems nor the financial resources to fix their year-2000 problems. But most at risk is the largest healthcare insurer in the United States—Medicare.

Just how big is Medicare?

- Medicare, through the Healthcare Financing Administration (HCFA), pays out over $200 billion in healthcare benefits each year.
- Medicare processes claims through a system of around 70 contractors.
- Medicare pays benefits through around 45 nationwide sites.
- Medicare serves approximately 38 million Americans.
- The Medicare system expects to process over one billion claims and pay $288 billion in benefits by the year 2000.
- The Medicare system pays claims submitted by hospitals, skilled nursing facilities, hospices, home health agencies, rehabilitation agencies, physicians, laboratories, equipment suppliers, and outpatient providers.

Source: Medicare Transaction System: Success Depends Upon Correcting Critical Managerial and Technical Weaknesses, Joel M. Willemssen, Government Accounting Office, May 16, 1997. Available at <http://www.access.gpo.gov/cgi-bin/getdoc.cgi?dbname=gao&docid=f:ai97078.txt.pdf>.

Big Systems—Big Problems

The Medicare system has been criticized for its lack of progress in preparing for the year-2000 problem. Part of the difficulty, of course, is that Medicare is a massive organization and year-2000 preparedness represents a monumental undertaking.

In May 1997, the Government Accounting Office (GAO) conducted an evaluation of Medicare's year-2000 preparations. A central issue is who should accept responsibility for fixing the problems. The Healthcare Financing Administration (HCFA), the agency responsible for managing Medicare, is holding contractors responsible, and the contractors are holding HCFA responsible.[7]

A further complication is the need to share and coordinate data among the various hospitals, providers, and the many Medicare contractors. This system has many points where information could be corrupted. Because of this interconnectedness, it would take only one non-compliant system to create a chain of errors with potentially far-reaching effects. Given the size of the organization, the scope of the project, and the fixed, immutable deadline, Medicare has a challenge unlike any it has ever faced.

Adding to HCFA's burden in dealing with its year-2000 problems has been the ongoing project of modernizing its many automated claims-processing and information systems. These projects have required tremendous financial and personnel resources—resources which have not been applied to the urgent year-2000 compliance problems.

In June of 1998, HCFA announced that at least one of these projects was "on hold until further notice"[8] due to the high demand for resources needed to fix HCFA's estimate of 49 million lines[9] of year-2000 non-compliant contractor code. Implementation of other modernization programs have likewise been delayed; however, some have voiced concern that additional resources may yet be needed to insure that enrollment systems continue to function and that beneficiaries are not denied services because their eligibility could not be confirmed.[10]

And these delays could be costly for Medicare patients. Originally scheduled for 1999, one of the delayed changes was a co-payment correction for Medicare patients. As a result, some patients could be paying 50% of their bills instead of 20% for at least another year, an estimated $570 million dollars out of patient's pockets.[11] Other delayed programs affecting patients include expanded coverage for the education and training of people with diabetes.[12]

Unfortunately, recent reports on the progress of HCFA in managing the changes at Medicare are not promising. A *New York Times* article on the upcoming GAO report added that not all Medicare systems are likely to be compliant in time.[13] This means that the delivery of benefits and services is likely to be interrupted as we head into the year 2000.

Street-Wide Testing

As noted earlier, the healthcare industry is enormous, accounting for about one-seventh of the economy. And it is complex, with numerous agencies that are reliant on each other, yet act independently. It should be a surprise to no one that the industry has lagged behind in its year-2000 preparations. According to a recent presentation on the problem to the U.S. Senate, a major handicap is that there is no single body or organization spearheading the year-2000 effort: "The U.S. health care community is a fragmented, diverse industry with no 'Big 3' or 'Big 6' to drive activity. There has been little or no coordination of Year 2000 activities and significant duplication of Year 2000 efforts."[14]

In other industries there is an emphasis on street-wide testing—making sure all the components function well together. This kind of focus and coordination could allow for the various components comprising the healthcare industry—practitioners, hospitals, insurance companies, and so on—to work together to make sure the system continues to function as a whole. But the lack of a central organizing force in healthcare makes street-wide testing unlikely.

The Last Word—Prescription for *You*

The healthcare industry exists to serve individuals in need, and it will continue to do so after the year 2000. But the year-2000 problem is putting strain on the fabric of the overall system, and we could feel the impact of that strain.

Timely Tips—Guidelines for the Millennium

You and your family's health is so very important this will be an area where you will want to be especially proactive in preparing for the year 2000. In order to adequately prepare, you will want to assess your needs.

1. Start the assessment process by making a list of all family members, be sure to include your parents if you are involved in their healthcare.
2. Next you will want to gather information on any medication requirements family members may have. Include:
   - both generic and brand names of all prescription medication
   - the precise dosages and how often they are taken or applied
   - common side effects
   - the name of the pharmaceutical company producing the medication. Most pharmacies will provide this information in written form whenever a prescription is filled. If not provided, ask for it.

Tips About Medication
   - Because you don't want to run out of important medications should there be disruptions in manufacturing or distribution, you may want to work

with your physician to ensure that you have a good supply on hand. If the drugs in question are not particularly dangerous, addictive, or require constant monitoring, most physicians will be willing to help. However, your insurance company may not be so willing to cooperate. Some plans restrict the amount of medication insurance companies will authorize at one time. If this is the case, you may be forced to pay for the prescription yourself.

- Some people will be tempted to stockpile medications by skipping doses and saving pills. This can be dangerous, and it would be reckless for anybody to advise such a course of action. Always work with your physician when it comes to making decisions about medication regimens.
- Many medications are available from more than one manufacturer. However, if any medications on your family's list come from a single source, you may want to ask your physician to provide a prescription, if possible, for a similar medication that is more readily obtainable. In addition, if a prescription is compounded specifically for someone, as natural hormone replacement may be, see if you can identity a second compounding pharmacy in case the first has year-2000 difficulties.
- Investigate your pharmacy's level of year-2000 readiness. Most pharmacies keep medication records on computers and refer to their databases for refills. Although federal law requires that pharmacies retain the original paper copy of your prescription, it may be stored away and require time to find. If you are not satisfied with your pharmacy's level of preparedness, consider doing business with one that takes year-2000 concerns seriously.
- Always check the dates used on the medication bottles. A missing four-digit date for the year may be a sign that a computer system is not year-2000 compliant. Because some dosage calculations are based on age, it is important to verify that the medications and dosages are correct. A year-2000 non-compliant computer could calculate your or a child's age incorrectly which could result in an incorrect dose of medication.

Tips About Medical Equipment

Does someone in your family use special medical equipment? If so, you should contact the manufacturer, not the distributor, to find out if your particular model is year-2000 compliant. A contact phone number or address for the manufacturer should be listed on the equipment, but if it is not, you can probably get this information from the local distributor. If you can't get a compliance assurance from the manufacturer, you may want to find an alternative device from a different manufacturer. Be sure to allow time to make needed changes.

If you are having trouble determining the year-2000 compliance of some piece of equipment, the Federal Drug Administration (FDA) or the Veteran's Administration (VA) may have information regarding its year-2000 compliance in the database they are collecting. You can find this information on these agencies Internet sites at <www.fda.org> or <www.va.org>

Even if your equipment is compliant, it probably will require electrical power, and in some instances, pure water. So it will be important to have auxiliary power and water supplies.

See Chapter 2,
*Power and Water
and the Year 2000.*

Ask in-home care providers about the compliance of any equipment they bring with them for use in treating you or someone in your family.

Planning for Level of Care

You can't always predict when you will need to use healthcare services—emergencies do happen. Nevertheless, you may be aware that some members of your family seem to need care more often than others. Some people rarely get sick, while others seem to move from one illness to the next. Often it is children or the elderly that fall into this latter category. If you have someone like this in your family, you need to make contingency plans. Will they require frequent visits to the doctor's office or hospital stays? Is it likely that their healthcare needs will increase as is often the case with older adults and those with chronic diseases? Some things to consider:

- Do you or those needing special care live independently but require frequent visitations? Are there family members or neighbors who can visit regularly should there be problems with communications or other services?
- If friends or family do not live nearby, is there community support, such as a church group, that can conduct regular status checks in the event of year-2000 problems?
- How do you or those needing extra care usually get to and from the doctor's office, hospital, pharmacy, laboratory, and so on? If public transportation is the primary means, what alternative methods of transportation can be set up ahead of time in case there are year-2000 complications?

- Have you developed a good relationship with a healthcare provider, medical doctor, or nurse who knows you and your condition?

Tips on Dealing With Healthcare Providers

Many healthcare practitioners depend heavily on the use of computers. How prepared is your doctor, chiropractor, acupuncturist, naturopath, or dentist to meet year-2000 challenges? Here are some questions to ask:

- What have you done to verify the equipment used in your practice is year-2000 compliant?
- What have you done to insure that electronic billing will be year-2000 compliant with agencies such as Medicare, Medicaid, and other insurance companies?
- Do you have hardcopy backups of my account showing my payments?
- How do you store my patient records, hardcopy or electronically?
- Is your appointment scheduling done via computer or hardcopy?

Investigate all entities with whom you regularly deal. Don't accept the answer that because a medical practice is small you don't need to worry about year-2000 problems. Small offices, especially medical practices, are no less likely than a large one to have problems with billing and equipment. All the concerns that have been discussed apply equally to any healthcare agency, clinic, or hospital that relies on computers.

In any event, one thing you will definitely want to do is obtain a hardcopy printout of all your medical records. Keep these where they are readily available. You may want to make backup copies of these important documents and store them in a safe place, such as a safe-deposit box. Keep your records up to date by requesting a copy of any additions to your medical file after each visit.

Insurance and Billing Tips

The healthcare you receive is often contingent on authorization for treatment from your insurance company, HMO, or Medicare. It is important for you to gather information about coverage. Make a list of insurance policy numbers, contact phone numbers, and deductible information for each family member. Read policies carefully so you are aware of covered services and exclusions.

You will want to know about the year-2000 health of your insurance company as well. If its computers are down, you may not be able to get authorization for services you need and your physician and hospital providing such services may not get paid.

Here are some questions to ask your insurance company:
- What progress have you made on your year-2000 program?
- What have you done to make sure that authorizations won't be affected by year-2000 problems?
- What contingency plans have you established in the event someone needs emergency care and the service providers can't verify benefits?
- What is the current estimated completion date for your company to fix its year-2000 problems?
- What are you doing to make certain the healthcare providers on your panel are year-2000 complaint and will continue to provide services?

Elective Surgeries and Procedures

Many medical procedures can't be anticipated ahead of time, but elective surgery can. If you are considering elective surgery, you may want to consider either moving the date of the procedure up, well ahead of the year 2000, or scheduling the procedure at least several weeks after the year 2000. By doing this, you are avoiding any year-2000 equipment failure concerns.

Be Prepared

In planning for the year-2000 problem and possible emergency situations, nothing is probably more appropriate than the Boy Scout motto—*be prepared*:
- Assemble a first aid kit. Information on assembling a kit is available at the Red Cross web site at <www.redcross.org>
- Know how to deal with emergency situations. For example, you may want to learn CPR, how to make a splint, bandage a burn, and so on. First aid and CPR classes are offered at hospitals and community health centers.

[1] Henderson, Mark. December 11, 1997. Millennium computer flaw 'may kill hospital patients'. *The Times Newspapers Limited.* Available at <http://www.Sunday-times.co.uk/news/pages/tim/97/12/11/timnws01027.html?1733620>

[2] Presentation to the U.S. Senate Special Committee on the Year 2000 Technology Problem, United States Senate, Presented by Joel M. Ackerman, Executive Director of Rx2000 Solutions Institute, July 23, 1998.

[3] DeBruce, Orlando. July 27, 1998. Y2K bug may infect VA Health. *Federal Computer Week.* Available at <http://www.fcw.com/pubs/fcw/1998/0727/fcw-newsva-7-27-98.htm>

[4] Statement to the Special Committee on the Year 2000 Problem, United States Senate, Re: Impact of the year 2000 problem on Physician Practices, Presented by Donald J. Palmisano, MD, JD, July 23, 1998, page 3.

[5] *Ibid.* page 4.

[6] Presentation to the U.S. Senate Special Committee on the Year 2000 Technology Problem, United States Senate, Presented by Joel M. Ackerman, Executive Director of Rx2000 Solutions Institute, July 23, 1998.

[7] Medicare Transaction System: Success Depends Upon Correcting Critical Managerial and Technical Weaknesses, Joel M. Willemssen, Government Accounting Office, May 16, 1997, GAO/AMD-97-78. Available at <http://www.access.gpo.gov/cgi-bin/getdoc.cgi?dbname=gao&docid=f:ai97078.txt.pdf>

[8] HCFA Announces MCS Conversion on Hold, EDI News Flash, Volume 1, issue 6, June, 1998.

[9] Testimony of Kevin Thurm, Deputy Secretary of Health and Human Services, U.S. Department of Health and Human Services, before the Senate Special Committee on the Year 2000 Technology Problem, July 23, 1998. page 5.

[10] *Ibid.*

[11] Computer trouble may cost medicare patients up to $570 million. September 1, 1998. *New York Times.* Available at <http://www12.nytimes.com/yr/mo/day/early/090198Y2K-medicare.html>

[12] Pear, Robert. September 27, 1998. Congress fears medicare will miss deadlines for change. *New York Times.* Available on the Internet at <http://www12.nytimes.com/library/politics/092798medicare.html>

[13] *Ibid.*

[14] Presentation to the U.S. Senate Special Committee on the Year 2000 Technology Problem, United States Senate, Presented by Joel M. Ackerman, Executive of Rx2000 Solutions Institute, July 23, 1998.

Chapter 5

Banking and Credit Cards and the Year 2000

In this chapter you will learn:

- How computer technology is used throughout the banking industry
- Who the financial regulators are and what they are doing to help the finance industry through the year-2000 problem
- How the year-2000 problem could affect checking and savings accounts
- What could happen when you borrow money from institutions
- About credit and debit cards and the year-2000 problem
- How your credit worthiness could be impacted by the year-2000 bug

In Banks We Trust . . .

Money. We spend a large part of our lives working to earn it—and an equivalent amount of time wishing we had more. And when we get more money, we worry about losing it. We are driven to earn money to take care of our families, our daily needs, our future security. Money is so ingrained in our way of thinking that it would be difficult, if not impossible, to spend a day not thinking about money in some way. Face it, money is on our minds.

Given the status of money in our culture, it should come as no surprise that certain events, such as the crash of 1929 and the Great Depression that followed, hold a special fascination, even reverence, in our psyches. While many of us have heard the stories about people jumping out of buildings after the stock market crash of 1929, few of us today really understand the hardships people endured when they lost their savings, houses, jobs, and other possessions. Similarly, few of us have experienced the stress caused by banks becoming insolvent. And even fewer understand the need to open *mattress accounts*, the practice of keeping money, gold, or jewelry hidden under the bedding, in a shoe box in the closet, or in a tin box buried in the barn.

We've had the great good fortune of being able to take for granted a monetary system that is safe and secure. The idea that banks might not be safe, that interest could be calculated incorrectly, or that payments might not be credited or considered overdue is uncommon thinking. We've become a secure and, perhaps, too complacent society. For some, the year-2000 problem could change that way of thinking.

Scoping the Problem—A Security Blanket in Shreds?

Consumer confidence is a phrase frequently bandied about in financial circles. The term speaks to the importance of people's perception of the banking system—and especially the security of the banking system. If you didn't trust that your bank were solid, would you keep your money in its vaults? Obviously, the answer is no. Consumer confidence is of such importance we have created institutions such as the Federal Deposit Insurance Corporation (FDIC) to stem concern of bank failure and avoid runs on banks. When it comes to the stability of the banking system, make no mistake, perception is reality. We *need* to believe in the stability of our banks—our belief is our security blanket.

Computers are an integral component of monetary institutions and the year-2000 bug could impact financial security. The same is true of the credit- and debit-card industry—which have also become a mainstay of our everyday reality.

The Banking Industry

It would be difficult to imagine a banking system that didn't rely on computers and specialized software programs. The banking industry was one of the first to begin the process of automating various tasks. Today, you can complete most of your banking needs without ever having to deal with a live person. Banking electronically is the latest activity processed via computer systems, and millions are beginning to discover the convenience of online banking. Before the advent of online banking, there was the automatic teller machine, or ATM as it is more commonly known. And before the ATM, there were large computer systems accounting for every penny spent and deposited. A lot has changed in the past several decades. Certainly, the banking industry today would not be capable of meeting our needs and expectations if it were not for computer hardware and software. Unfortunately, the dependence we have placed on these computer systems could come back to haunt us because of the year-2000 problem.

Financial institutions are facing three problems in solving their current and upcoming year-2000 problems.

First, financial institutions rely heavily on computer systems, either their own or those of other businesses contracted to provide services. Potential problems, if not evaluated and repaired, could include the inability to clear checks, errors in calculating interest and amortization of payments, direct deposit funds not being deposited, automated teller machines refusing to work, and vaults opening or not opening when they are supposed to.

Second, financial institutions must consider the computer systems that connect to their own. These systems include the wire-transfer systems, electronic data interchange systems, and electronic benefits transfer systems.

Finally, banks are increasingly concerned with another problem over which they have little control. Banks profit from making loans. And these profits are at risk if the companies borrowing money are not year-2000 compliant. The worst case scenario would be for banks to lose massive amounts of money from companies going bankrupt because they could not conduct business. As reported in the March 18, 1998 edition of the *Wall Street Journal*, banks are concerned that losses from bad loans could climb as a direct result of year-2000 problems. As a result, banks are beginning to ask borrowers for company information regarding year-2000 programs. The banks which are more vulnerable to problems from defaults are likely to be those that loan money to smaller businesses. Remember, small to moderate-size businesses are less likely to have a complete understanding of the year-2000 problems they face and the money to do something about it.

These problems are not to be taken lightly: Government watchdogs warn that as many as 700 banks could be forced to close their doors on Jan. 1, 2000, if their check-clearing software programs succumb to the "Millennium bug."[1]

This warning was issued by the Government Accounting Office (GAO) after a survey conducted by the Federal Deposit Insurance Corporation (FDIC) found that more than 200 banks were not doing enough to address their year-2000 problems, and that over 500 additional banks had not followed up with their third-party vendors and software providers to determine their year-2000 readiness.[2] In response, Senator Bob Bennett of Utah stated, "Unless more leadership and commitment are brought to bear on this problem, I fear a potential for financial chaos for many bank customers."[3]

Certainly, these warnings are frightening. There are approximately twenty-two thousand financial institutions across the United States with assets and deposits of approximately nine trillion dollars. Even a problem with only one percent of the daily dollar transactions could potentially be an error amounting to billions.

The year-2000 problem is costing banks a tremendous amount of money. Chase Manhattan was reported to spend about $200 to $250 million[4] to make sure their computer systems will operate into the next century; however, updated information indicates that Chase Manhattan's cost may be closer to $300 million.[5] Citicorp, in a recent SEC filing, disclosed that it will spend an estimated $600 million to fix its computer problems. A rule of thumb in the banking industry is that banks will need to spend $100,000 for every $100 million of assets to fix year-2000 problems.[6] Overall, it is expected that the 35 largest banks in the United States will spend an estimated $1.8 billion.[7] These costs are for making in-house computer systems compliant and verifying compliance with outside systems that banks must communicate with to conduct business. This includes verification of wire-transfer systems, automated clearing houses, check clearing providers, credit card merchants and issuing systems, automated teller machine networks, electronic data interchange systems and electronic benefits transfer systems.

Fortunately, the bigger banks have the resources and personnel with the skills to evaluate and fix their year-2000 problems. Unfortunately, smaller banks, such as community banks, may not be in this position.

Time Out!

In ancient Mesopotamia the gold standard was actually silver—a shekel was the monetary unit and weighted one-third of an ounce, or about the weight of three pennies. You could buy just about anything using shekels. A quart of barley cost three-hundredths of a shekel, or you could get someone to work for you for one month for one shekel. Once a silver standard was in place, a price could be put on lots of things. If you lived in the city of Eshnuuna around 2000 BC and had trouble controlling your temper, you could be fined 60 shekels for biting another man's nose, or 10 shekels for slapping another in the face.

Source: Pringle, Heather. The cradle of cash.Vol.19, Discover Magazine, 10-01-1998,pp 52(8).

The Financial Regulators

There are five government agencies that are responsible for guidance and supervision of the nation's 22,000 financial institutions, collectively referred to as the Federal Financial Institutions Examination Council (FFIEC). The five agencies are the Federal Reserve Board, Office of the Comptroller of the Currency (OCC), Federal Deposit Insurance Corporation (FDIC), Office of Thrift Supervision (OTS), and the National Credit Union Association (NCUA). Together, these agencies are responsible for maintaining safety and soundness through assessing these financial institutions progress in mitigating year-2000 risks.

Agency	Approximate number of finanical institution supervised	Dollar Amount
Federal Reserve Board	992 State-chartered member banks and bank holding companies	$1.2 trillion in assets
Office of the Comptroller of the Currency (OCS)	2,600 Federally-chartered national banks	$2.9 trillion in assets
Federal Deposit Insurance Committee (FDIC)	6,200 state-chartered non-member banks Also serves as the insurer of approximately 11,000 banks and savings institutions	$1 trillion in assets $2.7 trillion insured deposits
Office of Thrift Supervision (OTS)	1,200 savings and loan institutions (thrifts)	$770 billion in assets
National Credit Union Association (NCUA)	11,000 federally- and state-chartered credit unions	$345 billion in assets

Source: Federal Regulatory Efforts to Ensure Financial Institution Systems are Year 2000 Compliant, Testimony before the Committee on Banking and Financial Services, House of Representatives, Statement of Jack L. Brock, March 24, 1998. Available from the GAO web site at <http://www.goa.com>.

These agencies, acting collectively under the auspices of the FFIEC, began addressing the year-2000 problem in June 1996 by formally alerting financial institutions to risks posed by the year-2000 problem.[8] Since that time, the FFIEC has increasingly monitored progress of its member financial institutions. An initial assessment completed at the end of 1997 concluded that over 5,000 institutions were not adequately addressing their year-2000 risks—nearly 23% of all financial institutions in the United States.[9]

At the request of the Committee on Banking and Financial Services, the General Accounting Office (GOA) provided information regarding problems the FFIEC has or is likely to have in successfully addressing year-2000 challenges. Per the report, the GAO reported that:

- *All* agencies in the FFIEC were behind in assessing individual institution's Y2K readiness, principally due to starting late. While the Office of Management and Budget (OMB) and the GAO recommended the initial assessment be complete by the summer of 1997, the FFIEC did not complete the assessment until November/December 1997. The GAO report stated that, because of this delay, "the time available for assessing institutions' progress during renovation, validation, and implementation phases and for taking needed corrective actions is compressed."[10]
- The GAO also reported that the FFIEC was not collecting all the necessary data needed to determine in which phase of correction institutions were.
- The GAO criticized the FFIEC for not yet having developed key guidance for its institutions to use in developing and correcting their problems, including contingency plans to mitigate potential disruptions related to year-2000 problems.
- Finally, the GAO was concerned that the FFIEC lacked the technical resources and trained staff necessary to adequately evaluate the full scope of year-2000 problems, from identification to conversion efforts. As a result, "the risk of noncompliance by institutions and service bureaus—and the government's exposure to losses—is significantly increased."[11]

The FFIEC faces significant challenges as the year 2000 approaches. It will be important to quickly identify any and all institutions that will not meet the year-2000 deadline. This is necessary to determine future enforcement action, ranging from increased supervision to monetary penalties. As the deadline approaches, regulatory evaluations will increase in complexity, and the strain of trying to meet these demands with an already small pool of technical resources will grow.

Personal Banking

Most of us don't think much about how the trillions of dollars trading hands each day get from point A to point B. We do care, however, about making sure our checks are correctly debited and payments to us correctly credited. A principle issue in exploring the year-2000 problem is the potential impact on normal, daily banking. Even some of the more common banking transactions, such as writing checks, paying mortgages, and maintaining the correct balance in our accounts, may be affected.

Time Out!

A Pocket full of -Ouch! Trade was much easier once money was invented. Precious metals were used around the world as a medium of exchange, but how would people know they were getting the real thing? How could a person be confident the lump of metal being offered for cloth was really silver, not a cheaper alloy? What was needed was a method of certification—enter the government. Around 600 BC, the kings of China certified their money with inscriptions stating the place of origin and the weight, and shaped these small pieces of bronze in the form of tiny knives and spades. Round coins came later.

Source: Pringle, Heather. The cradle of cash.Vol.19, Discover Magazine, 10-01-1998,pp 52(8).

Checking

Have you ever thought about the life of a check? Most of us don't think twice after writing one. Just how does money get from one account to another? While the U.S. government wrote a detailed, 156-page guide to on the subject, a brief paragraph will have to suffice here.[12]

When you write a check paying for your grocery-store purchase, the store sends your check to its bank to be credited to its account. If the grocery store uses the same bank as you do, it's easy—money is transferred from your account to the store's (via computer systems, of course). If more than one bank is involved, the grocery store's bank sends your check to its regional Federal Reserve Bank which serves as a clearinghouse for the millions of checks received each day from various banks. The Federal Reserve Bank then credits the grocery store's bank for payment while sending your check to your bank where your account is debited. In this case where there are two Federal Reserve Banks involved, the first flies your check to the second, where it is returned to your bank, and then back to you in your month-end statement.

This system relies on the efficiency and accuracy of computer systems, so the need for year-2000 compliant systems is obvious. If the payment and clearinghouse system is not year-2000 compliant, the potential disaster would be enormous. The entire process could come to a grinding halt. It would certainly not be possible for checks to be cleared as rapidly as they are if we had to return to the days when the process was conducted by hand, one check at a time.

Fortunately, the most recent news coming from the Federal Reserve System indicates good progress towards correcting their own year-2000 related problems. In a recent interview, a Federal Reserve executive stated that the Federal Reserve Banking and Clearinghouse system was year-2000 compliant with their newly revamped computer systems to go online in July 1998.[13]

It is important to remember that the Federal Reserve is charged with two responsibilities when considering year-2000 problems. First, the Reserve itself must be internally compliant to inter-operate with banks using its clearinghouse systems. Second, the Reserve is responsible for supervising the year-2000 compliance progress for over 992 state-chartered member banks and bank holding companies. In case you're curious, these 992 member banks and holding companies currently are responsible for $1.2 trillion in assets.[14]

Finally, because there is an interdependency between different sectors of the economy (banking required telecommunications and electricity, for example) it may be wise to take reports of year-2000 compliance with caution. Therefore, it is in your best interest to take action in the event there is a glitch along the way.

Borrowing and Lending

Interested in buying a new home for your growing family? How about that sleek, new sports car?

Millions of borrowers have loans and mortgages which are managed by computers—computers that figure interest, send payment notices, and credit accounts. If your payment is late, a computer determines the late-payment fees and sends you a notice. All of these functions are date dependent and have the potential for being impacted if year-2000 problems are not evaluated and corrected.

In November 1997, a bank computer alerted staff that a business loan was more than 90 years overdue.[15] The problem? The loan payments were scheduled through the year 2003, and apparently, a computer system along the way thought payment was due in 1903. Thankfully, the problem was caught and corrected before a notice was sent to the customer. However, this is an excellent example of how the year-2000 problem can impact individuals.

ATMs, Credit, and Debit Cards

In August 1997, the first year-2000 related lawsuit was filed by a grocery store against a manufacturer of cash registers. Reportedly, people with credit cards expiring in and after the year 2000 became angry when their cards were rejected by the cash register and credit card point-of-service computer system. This left store owners with no choice but to handle credit card transactions the old fashioned way—by hand.

For more information as to how the year-2000 problem could affect grocery stores, see Chapter 2, *Food and the Year 2000.*

Adding to the problem, a cash register didn't just deny someone's credit card, but caused all ten of the checkout line registers to crash simultaneously, leaving everyone stuck until the computer system was revived. The store owner reported that the entire computerized checking system crashed over 100 times.[16]

If you take out all your credit cards and look at the expiration dates, you will probably notice that few, if any, have dates that expire after 1999. There is a very good reason for this. Credit card companies found that there were simply too many problems occurring with these cards. Many people found their cards being rejected, leaving them confused, angry, and even embarrassed. Business owners faced the prospect of losing customers who might choose never to return. For these reasons, a number of major credit card merchant banks stopped producing and releasing credit and debit cards expiring after the year 1999. While the problem has reportedly been fixed, some critics remain skeptical for reasons you will see later in this chapter.

Just how big is the credit-card industry?

- In 1997, Visa International reported that consumers worldwide purchased $1 *trillion* in goods and services via the Visa card, an all time high.[18] MasterCard reported a very respectful $550 billion for 1996.
- Visa reported having more than 572 million credit and debit cards in use around the world as of March, 1997.
- MasterCard reported handling more than 7.5 million transactions each day.[19]
- MasterCard reported international transactions numbering about 6 *billion* transactions for 1996.
- Visa and MasterCard reported their respective cards are accepted at more than 380,000 and 350,000 ATMs worldwide.

Source: Visa and MasterCard

Time Out!

Necessity has been credited with being the mother of invention—in this case, paper money was the invention. During the late 1600s when part of Canada was still under French rule, there was a severe shortage of coins. When the ships arrived from France, the settlers paid for French goods with their carefully hoarded coins—so in general the movement of coinage was back to France. Each summer a government ship sailed for Canada with coin to pay the troops. In 1685, the ship was delayed for eight months and the soldiers had no pay. The desperate Governor came up with a brilliant idea: he requisitioned all decks of playing cards in the colony, cut each card into four pieces, wrote a monetary value on each, and signed and stamped them. He then ordered that these cards be used as payment for any goods or services with no changes in price— and the merchants accepted them! When the boat arrived in January, the pieces of cards were exchanged at par for the coins, then the cards were destroyed.

Source: http://www.micheloud.com/FXM/MH/canada.htm

Compared to the various forms of paper and coin money systems that have existed for many thousands of years, the use of credit cards, debit cards, and Automatic Teller Machine (ATMs) are relatively new. The first *official* credit card was issued by The Franklin National Bank in New York in 1951.[17] This industry has grown at an amazing pace over the past 30 years so that now almost everyone in the United States has a credit or debit card, and most of us have several. Convenience has been the main spur to this growth. Credit cards are easy to use, light to carry, and above all, fast. They also afford greater security if lost or stolen. And if you travel overseas, credit card companies handle the exchange rates so you don't have to.

Given these astounding figures, along with the ever increasing use of ATMs, the potential for year-2000 problems is great.

How the Credit Card Industry Works

It is a commonly held misconception that the major credit card companies, such as Visa and MasterCard, are responsible for issuing credit and debit cards. While this is true for some credit cards, it is *not* true for Visa and MasterCard. These two companies license their names to members, but do not issues cards, set fees, or establish the interest rate of your cards. This is done by the banks that license the Visa or MasterCard brand name.

Visa and MasterCard by themselves, therefore, can't solve the year-2000 problems affecting credit and debit cards. Recognizing they have a vested interest in the smooth operation of the network in the year 2000, Visa and MasterCard have offered guidance to member banks and merchants. But in fact, Visa and MasterCard have little to do with much of the equipment, including devices known as Point-of-Service (POS) terminals that are used to read and ask for authorization based on the information on the magnetic strip on your card. It is ultimately up to the merchants who accept credit cards and the device manufacturers to insure that their systems, from the chips inside the POS terminals to the software and computer systems that authorize, monitor, and track transactions, are year-2000 compliant. All credit card companies, therefore, have to work with those banks that have contracted with them, as well as third-party vendors, in order for the system to be year-2000 compliant.

Of course, since credit card services require the use of telecommunications lines and electricity, there is a need for these utilities to be year-2000 ready as well. In truth, the credit- and debit-card system is a vast network of interconnected devices all of which must be ready for the year 2000 for you to use your cards.

Like all other possible year-2000 problems, the potential domino effect could turn a minor annoyance into a major headache. For example, last May, 1,529 ATM's in Northern California were shutdown for a two-hour period.[20] Miles away at an electrical substation, a simple human error resulted in a power shut down to the bank's data processing center. Not only did the bank's ATMs go off line, but its entire online telecommunications system was out of service as well. While this event was not the result of year-2000 problems, it does illustrate how interdependent the service systems are. If *everything* doesn't work as planned, no *part* is safe.

If you want to use your card while traveling overseas for business or a vacation, experts in the industry are even more hesitant about year-2000 readiness. It just isn't known how year-2000 problems will impact card users outside of the United States, especially in technologically less sophisticated areas of the world.

The year-2000 status of the industry continues to evolve. Visa and MasterCard recently authorized their member banks to deliver cards with expiration dates past the year 2000 to folks like you and me. These new

For information on how the year-2000 problem could affect power or telecommunications, see Chapters 2 and 7.

For information about Travel, see Chapter 10, *Travel and the Year 2000.*

cards were approved only after a two-year period of testing that involved issuing several hundred thousand test cards to employees. Despite signs of progress, some remain skeptical, believing that the magnitude and complexity of the year-2000 problems facing the credit- and debit-card industry will simply not allow for a smooth transition into the year 2000.

Your Credit Report

An important, yet overlooked and misunderstood aspect of buying a car, home, or even getting a credit card is your credit report. As many have unfortunately discovered, poor credit makes it difficult to borrow the money needed for many things. Your credit worthiness is your license to participate in this great consumer society we live in.

Years ago, when you wanted to borrow money from a bank, your credit worthiness was determined by the relationship you had with your banker. The same was true for retail stores that would allow buying on credit. However, after World War II, the need for consumer credit grew, and a uniform system of reporting credit information evolved. Eventually, a number of agencies consolidated, leaving the three large consumer reporting agencies we have today:[21] Equifax, Experian, and Trans-Union

The types of information stored by consumer reporting agencies have also undergone change over time. Initially, these agencies only collected negative information about people, based primarily on non payment of bills. Over time, these agencies began collecting additional information, both positive and negative. The introduction of computer technology allowed the agencies to collect and analyze vast amounts of information.[22]

Today, the three large consumer reporting agencies have collected and analyzed literally billions of pieces of information. This information, as well as public-record information, is provided to consumer reporting agencies by many sources that offer credit, including banks, mortgage companies, credit unions, automobile dealers, and collection agencies.[23] One of these agencies collects information on 1.8 billion consumer accounts *per month*.[24] Further, the same agency has collected information on 160 million persons and 105-110 million households.[25] Some of this information is then sold back to those who want to evaluate your credit worthiness.

The information recorded about you in consumer agency files can be extensive, more than what you might expect. Information about you can include:[26]

- Telephone numbers
- Date of birth
- Social security numbers
- Current automobile loans
- Current mortgage information
- Student loan information
- Head of household information
- Marital status
- Credit amounts on all open loans
- What bank cards you have
- How long you have lived in a particular place
- Whether you have bought from particular mail order companies

This is only a partial list. The likelihood is great that at least one of the three consumer reporting agencies has some information about you. Of course, all this information is reported, stored, and analyzed via computers. It is important that this information be accurate. And to keep it accurate, all the computer systems providing information to the consumer reporting agencies from banks, credit unions, and the like must be evaluated for their year-2000 compliance and repaired as necessary. In addition, the computer systems *storing* these billions of pieces of information must also be year-2000 compliant.

The Last Word—Laughing All the Way to the Bank?

Money is a critically important topic in our society. It is the means by which we obtain the basic necessities of daily life, such as food, clothing, and shelter. That is why it is important that every company and government agency having anything to do with the handling of our hard-earned money be year-2000 compliant. However, it is equally important that we have an understanding of what happens to our money, *and* to our credit, so we can be prepared ourselves. Only then can we continue to laugh our way to the bank.

Timely Tips—Guidelines for the Millennium

Money and money management are likely to be of great concern as we move into the next century. After food and water, money and the security it offers is often among the primary considerations people have in times of crisis.

There are a number of things people can do to prepare for the coming of the millennium. When evaluating your options, the first item of business is to assess the year-2000 readiness of your banking institution and its ability to continue to provide the services you require.

Security of Your Banking Institution

It is important to evaluate the year-2000 preparedness of *all* the financial institutions with which you deal—credit unions or savings and loans, banks, and so on. Use the following questions as a guide to gather this information.
- What is the bank doing to prepare its computers for the year 2000?
- What is the anticipated impact of the year-2000 computer problem on the bank?
- How can I be satisfied that this bank will be ready on time?
- What is the bank's schedule for fixing and testing its systems? What progress has been made on this schedule thus far? Are copies of this schedule available for review?
- Can I receive a recent company report or other public statement in which the company discusses its approach to the year-2000 problem?
- What assurance do I have that my accounts, loans, interest calculation, and so on will not be affected by the year-2000 problem?
- Are my funds FDIC insured?
- What is the status of the bank's check-clearing systems and credit-card handling systems?
- Does the bank have an estimate of how much it is going to cost to repair year-2000 problems, and are there sufficient funds allocated to cover the cost?

General Considerations

Even if your bank has a good year-2000 plan in place, there are some other factors to consider when evaluating the potential effect of the year-2000 on your bank. While there are no guarantees as to an institution's ability to contend with global year-2000 problems, taking the following factors into consideration can provide some additional security as we head into the year 2000.
- Bigger is probably better. Bigger institutions are more likely to have the funds, personnel and knowledge available to fix year-2000 problems than are smaller ones.

- Other factors are important too, such as the degree of overseas loan exposure.[27] For this information, ask for a copy of the banks annual report or ask an officer of the bank how to obtain this information. The fewer loans and investments made overseas the better because there is great concern with overseas year-2000 progress in general.[28]
- The more cash the bank has on hand the better.[29] This means that the institution is more likely to recover if it is holding loans to businesses that fail due to year-2000 problems.

To Protect Your Assets

There are no guarantees when considering issues related the year-2000 problem. Even if you believe your financial institution is making good progress with its year-2000 plan, you need to stay informed. There are several things you can do to protect your assets and your access to them. Things to consider include:

- Having your deposits in FDIC-insured accounts provide some degree of safety, even though this doesn't guarantee immediate access to your funds, should a bank close due to year-2000 problems.
- Overseas banks with no U.S. branches are a big question mark in terms of fund availability. While you are probably close to any number of bank branches, if there are telecommunications problems due to year-2000 problems, access to your funds may be more difficult. It is also not clear if funds are insured in foreign institutions.
- Keep a paper trail of all your account activity, including debits and credits. In the event your account records are lost or corrupted, you will have records to establish your account balance.
- It may be wise to have a certain amount of cash on hand in case check-clearing and credit-card systems are interrupted. This will allow you to make purchases if other methods of payment can't be used. And, you will be able to continue making timely payments on your own obligations such as car loans, credit cards and the mortgage.
- Remember that money you keep at your home is not insured. If it is lost or stolen, it is gone. Consider a safe-deposit box or a fire-proof safe.
- If your paycheck is deposited electronically, find out if your company has tested the electronic deposit systems for year-2000 compliance. Does your company have a contingency plan in the event there are problems?

• If you are concerned that year-2000 problems have the potential to create more serious and long-lasting financial disruptions, you may want to have alternative forms of money, such as precious metals or coins, as part of your year-2000 plan. Talk to your investment advisor for more information about these options.

Credit cards

The use of plastic to pay for purchases has become a standard practice. Although the credit-card industry is reasonably sure that it has resolved or minimized year-2000 problems with the acceptance of cards, there are still some steps you can take to further minimize any year-2000 difficulties.

• Having several credit cards from different merchant banks increases the likelihood that you have a card from a bank whose system is year-2000 compliant.

• A credit card with an expiration date prior to the year 2000 is less likely to be rejected by a non-compliant system. Having such a card can provide peace of mind until the year 2000, especially if you travel overseas where year-2000 progress is more questionable.

Loans/Mortgages

Banks provide many services beyond checking and savings accounts. If you have loans or a mortgage, you will want to monitor the accuracy of these accounts. As we head into the year 2000, one of the important safety steps you can take is to obtain hard copies of all these loan agreements and the activity on these accounts. A paper record of these accounts and their payment histories allows you to:

• Prove you have an account
• Show payments, credits, and so on
• Check to see if interest has been calculated incorrectly after the year 2000.

Protecting your credit record

It is equally important these days to protect your credit history. Most people have never asked for a copy of their credit report, but it is wise to do so. As part of your financial year-2000 plan, you will want to monitor your credit history and be able to show, via hard copies, you have a good credit record. Following are the phone numbers and web addresses for the three major consumer credit reporting agencies:

- Equifax - 1-800-685-1111 - http://www.equifax.com
- Experian - 1-800-682-7654 and 1-888-397-3742 - http://www.experian.com
- Trans-Union - 1-800-888-4213 - http://www.transunion.com

---

[1] Glass, Andrew, J. February 11, 1998. "Millennium bug" could close banks. *The Atlanta Journal-Constitution.* Available at <http://www.accessatlanta.com/business/news/1998/02/11/2000.html>

[2] GAO Testimony before the subcommittee on Financial Services and Technology, Committee on Banking, Housing, and Urban Affairs, U.S. Senate, Year 2000 Crisis: Federal Deposit Insurance Corporation's Efforts to Ensure Bank Systems Are Year 2000 Compliant, Statement of Jack L. Brock, Jr. February 10, 1998.

[3] Same as one above.

[4] Mead, Wendy S. April 1997. Chase projects $250M to avert year 2000 glitches. *American Banker*, Vol. CLXII No. 69. Available at <http://www.americanbanker.com>

[5] Luhby, Tami. March 13, 1998. Stocks: Year-2000 expenses climb, but analysts undaunted. *American Banker*, Series 13. Available at <www.americanbanker.com>

[6] Kline, Alan. February 17, 1998. Small banks' year-2000 budgets "Way to Low." *American Banker.* Available at <http://www.americanbanker.com>

[7] The Wall Street Journal Electronic Edition, Banks Worry Year 2000 Woes May Lead To Rise in Bad Loans, Rick Brooks, March 18, 1998. Available at <http://www.wsj.com>

[8] Federal Regulatory Efforts to Ensure Financial Institution Systems are Year 2000 Compliant, Testimony before the Committee on Banking and Financial Services, House of Representatives, Statement of Jack L. Brock, March 24, 1998. Available from the GAO web site at <http://www.goa.com>

[9] *Ibid.*

[10] *Ibid.*

[11] *Ibid..*

[12] Payments, Clearance, and Settlement: A Guide to the Systems, Risks, and Issues. Report to the Chairman Committee on Banking and Financial Services, House of Representatives, June 1997. Available at <http://www.access.gpo.gov/cgi-bin/getdoc.cgi?dbname=gao&docid=f:gg97073.txt.pdt.>

[13] Chambers, Rob. July 15. Y2K dilemma no problem for Fed, exec says, *The Atlanta Constitution*.

[14] Federal Regulatory Efforts to Ensure Financial Institution Systems are Year 2000 Compliant, Testimony before the Committee on Banking and Financial Services, House of Representatives, Statement of Jack L. Brock, March 24, 1998. Available from the GAO web site at <http://www.goa.com>

[15] Gruber, William. November 19, 1997. Banks brace for millennium bug bite. *Chicago Tribune*.

[16] Wong, Wylie. August 18, 1997. Grocer registers year 2000 suit. *Computerworld*. Available at <http://www.computerworld.com>

[17] MasterCard International. Available at <http://www.mastercard.com>

[18] Visa International. Available at <http://www.visa.com>

[19] MasterCard International, Consolidated Financial Information report. Available at <http://www.mastercard.com>

[20] Sinton, Peter. May 14, 1998. B of A ATM's crash for 2 hours. *San Francisco Chronicle*.

[21] United States of America, Before Federal trade Commission, Initial Decision of the Honorable James P. Timony, In the Matter of Trans Union Corporation. Available at <http://www.ftc.gov/os/1998/9808/index.htm#26>, page 4.

[22] *Ibid.*

[23] *Ibid.* page 5.

[24] *Ibid.*

[25] page 6.

[26] *Ibid.* pages 5-13.

[27] Keyes, Tony. 1997. The year 2000 computer crisis: an investors survival guide. *The Y2K Investor*. p.46.

[28] *Ibid.*

[29] *Ibid.*

Chapter 6

Investment and the Year 2000

In this chapter you will learn:

- About computer technology in the stock markets
- About problems people had in contacting brokers during previous periods of market volatility
- About trading companies' efforts to fix year-2000 problems
- What one economist has estimated the odds of a global recession to be in the year 2000
- What the Securities and Exchange Commission (SEC) has done to protect investors and what information companies will be required to provide as a result
- About IRAs, 401Ks, mutual funds and the year-2000 problem

No Longer a Game for Just the Rich

Whether a lock box hidden in the closet or a diverse portfolio of stocks, bonds, and other sophisticated investment vehicles, the actions we take with our hard-earned money represent our hopes and dreams for the future. As such, we are investors. However, many people are investors who may not think of themselves as such. Anybody participating in employee benefit plans, which frequently offer choices of mutual funds or other investment options, is as much an investor as the person who reads the financial news and buys stock directly through a broker. So, too, is the individual who buys government treasury notes or bonds and files them away in a safe-deposit box.

The investment world of today is very different than it was even ten years ago. The impact of technology in this area has been tremendous, so much so that even the small investor can participate in making investment decisions that, just a few years ago, were reserved for the wealthy. More people making their own investment decisions in combination with the immense technological infrastructure now in place make it essential to explore any impact the year-2000 computer problem may introduce. Any negative impact could be more far reaching than ever before.

Scoping the Problem—Hang on for the Ride

As with any exploration of the year-2000 problem, there are several levels or facets to explore in getting a *big-picture* understanding of what we are facing. It's only with this broad understanding that we can make informed decisions— an essential element in dealing with whatever potential risk we may encounter entering the next millennium.

It seems there are few experts taking the middle ground when the words *money* and *year 2000* are used in combination. Most experts take one of the two extremes—that the year 2000 is going to be a minor annoyance at worst, or that the year 2000 will be the financial downfall of the world resulting in civil unrest and anarchy. The fact of the matter is *nobody* really knows the full impact that the year-2000 problem will have, making it all that much more important to take prudent, defensive action now.

There are at least four areas needing examination in determining the risk to our investments:
- the infrastructure of the market-trading systems (What is the ability of the exchange markets and other financial institutions to continue doing business?)
- the companies in which you invest (What is the likelihood these companies will or will not be impacted by the year-2000 problem? In other words, if business goes out of business, there is no business for the trading business!)
- the most typical types of personal investments (What might be the impact to the most common types of investment vehicles, such as mutual funds, stocks, bonds, 401Ks, IRAs, and the like. *Note: Other financial investments are beyond the scope of this book.*)
- investment strategies to help prepare for whatever the year-2000 problem may present (What criteria should be considered in developing a plan of action with investments?)

Market Infrastructure

From an investor's point of view, the infrastructure can be defined as all points with which we interact when investing funds in the securities industry. And the securities industry is large, including some 4,950 registered investment companies in 1,100 investment company complexes, 7,500 registered investment advisors, 8,300 registered broker-dealers, 1,248 registered transfer agents, and 24 self-regulatory organizations and clearing agencies.[1]

The dollar amounts involved, too, are staggering. Investment advisors alone manage approximately $13 trillion in savings for families in the United States. Mutual funds control over $5 trillion in assets, of which an estimated 35%, or approximately $1.75 trillion, are the assets of retirement plans.[2]

When financial people make reference to *the market*, they are referring to the various exchanges where investors, ranging from the single individual to institutional investors such as insurance companies, buy and sell everything including stocks, bonds, options, and commodities. Generally, when people use the term *market* they are referring to the stock market, where shares of companies are traded. The largest of these markets include exchanges such as the New York Stock Exchange (NYSE) and the Nasdaq, operated by the National Association of Securities Dealers (NASD). While these exchanges are familiar names, there are many other exchanges in the United States and across the world that are not so commonly known.

The volume of trading on these exchanges is mind boggling—the numbers so large that they become meaningless because they go beyond our comprehension levels. The Nasdaq, for example, reported an average daily share volume of 626.8 *million* shares per day as of September 30, 1997.[3]

Is the trading spirit just limited to humans? Experimenters at the Yerkes Regional Primate Center found that chimpanzees want to trade, too. The experimenter would point to an object inside a chimp's cage and hold out a piece of food such as an apple or a banana. About half of the chimps learned to make the trade. The more desirable the food, the quicker the response. Once they got the trading concept, shrewd chimp traders began to negotiate on their own terms, refusing to a trade unless given the particular food desired.

Time Out!

Source: Pringle, Heather. The cradle of cash.(types of money and usage of money historically)(Cover Story)., Vol.19, Discover Magazine, 10-01-1998,pp 52(8).

The National Association of Securities Dealers (NASD), the parent of Nasdaq, also reported trading 138.1 *billion* shares in 1996 on the Nasdaq in comparison to the impressive 104.6 *billion* shares traded in 1996 on the NYSE.[4] These numbers have been growing by leaps and bounds year after year, and they are expected to continue to do so.

The sophistication of the computer system technology used to handle the incredible volume of these exchanges is equally impressive. Somewhere, a computer system keeps track of every trade, the time of the transaction, who bought, who sold, and how much. Both the Nasdaq and the NYSE use computer and telecommunications systems allowing, for all practical purposes, instantaneous trading. The NYSE uses two computer centers (one for backup) filled with 450 refrigerator-sized computers connected by hundreds of miles of fiber-optic cable, synchronized by two atomic-clocks.[5] Similarly, the Nasdaq has invested hundreds of millions of dollars in their systems. And, according to a paper regarding their technology, the Nasdaq computers are reported to be capable of trading *one billion* shares per day.[6]

Market Drivers

Investor perception can play a large role in the direction stock markets move. On the news we hear reports of the number of points, up or down, the market was for any particular day. Some even keep up with the stock market on a per-minute basis. But rather than an indicator of current economic conditions, the market is considered by many to reflect things to come in about six months. That is, the stock market forecasts what might happen several months down the road. It is this perception of the stock market's future performance that is one of the driving factors making prices change today.

If the market is driven by fear—emotion rather than reason—we can see periods of rapid selling with increasing volume (numbers of shares being sold). Escalating investor anxiety can drive the market further down, adding momentum to the decline of share prices.

On October 28, 1997, Nasdaq registered a record 1.375 billion trades as the market rebounded from a record point loss just the day before. Similarly, the NYSE registered a record number of shares traded, 1.2 billion shares. The experience that traders had during this period of instability can provide useful information in our preparation for the coming of the year 2000. Just what were some of the difficulties experienced?

- Many people found they could not contact their brokers by phone. There were reports of people trying for hours, getting one busy signal after another.
- Some people even went to their local broker's office, only to find the brokers were also hampered by an inability to communicate directly with trading computer systems.
- Those that did get through the busy phone lines found themselves spending a very long time on hold. And, after placing an order to buy or sell, many reported that they could not get confirmation of their trade as some computer systems, on at least one of the major markets, were backed up to the point that it took many hours to confirm trades.
- People who traded via the Internet didn't find it much easier as this form of communication also uses telephone lines. Internet trading was also slowed by the way the Internet routes information over the labyrinth of telephone lines and computers. According to one report, an individual trying to trade via her online service found her request had to be routed through 18 different networks before reaching the broker.[7]
- There were problems with the big, sophisticated computer systems as well. A Nasdaq computer used for updating stock prices stopped working at 3:17 p.m. and did not send confirmations until hours later.[8]

These markets are highly computerized, interconnected networks relying on the smooth functioning of all the parts. Like a chain, a network is only as strong as its weakest link. Therefore, it's up to everyone involved in the trading chain to make certain their systems are capable of conducting business, especially during crucial times when it is most important.

When Alexander the Great conquered the Persian Empire in 330 BC, he found 1000 tons of gold and silver ingots in the treasury, and 250 tons of gold coins. The ingots were melted down and coins were minted. These were used to pay the troops and given as rewards to loyal followers. So vast was the amount of money distributed that these coins were used throughout the enormous empire he had created, which stretched from Greece to India. These coins were the first truly international currency.

Time Out!

Source: Milton Meltzer, Gold. Harper Collins Publishers, 1993, page 20.

The exchanges and brokerage firms appear to have taken these difficult trading days to heart and have been upgrading their systems to better handle momentous events in the market. And specifically, major players have been preparing their systems for the year 2000 by running mock trading, simulating Friday, December 1999 and January 3, 2000 trading (January 3rd is the first day of trading in the year 2000). Additional, comprehensive testing is planned for Spring 1999, and will include even more brokerages.

Thus far, the results of the limited testing appear promising. The first test, conducted July 1998, involved 29 securities firms and 13 stock markets and utilities. The Securities Industry Association (SIA), a firm helping to manage this year-2000 testing, reported that preliminary feedback from the testing showed that the infrastructure was sound but that there were a few incidents, including some trades being sent to the incorrect exchange and computers not recognizing valid test symbols.[9]

Although this preliminary test didn't include many smaller securities firms or international markets and was restricted to a single geographical location, it's reassuring that the financial sector is working hard to fix their year-2000 problems.[10] All told, Wall Street firms are expected to spend between four and six billion dollars to address year-2000 problems. Still, it can be argued that much more testing needs to be conducted as a single test, even a successful one, is not indicative of having solved all year-2000 bugs.

Per a June 1998 Securities and Exchange Commission (SEC) report on industry progress, there is still much work ahead.[11] While the majority of mission-critical systems had been assessed and approximately 73% to 84% had begun the process of fixing these important systems, only 26% to 29% had completed the process of fully implementing necessary changes.

Mission Critical Systems being repaired

	Assessment	Remediation	Testing	Implementation
Exchange and NASD	99.2%	73.1%	51.7%	26%
Clearing Agency	100%	83.6%	62.9%	28.6%

Source: from the second SEC report on the Readiness of the US Securities Industry, June 1998.

Stocks/Companies

The effect of the year-2000 problem on investments in businesses through the purchase of stocks, bonds, and so on, is another important issue to explore.

The health of businesses, often gauged by their revenue, plays an important role in the direction of the financial markets. Remember that investors attempt to anticipate *future* earnings and revenue of these businesses. You will also want to carefully monitor your own investments, whether it is done through the direct purchasing of stocks or mutual funds via your company retirement plan.

Someone once said that *the business of the United States is business*. This statement serves to emphasize how our economy and quality of life depends of the continued functioning of the economic model that has materially served us so well. Therefore, the readiness of the many businesses in the United States and across the world in tackling the year-2000 issue is of serious concern. It is an issue further emphasized by the estimate of Ed Yardeni, director of Deutsche Bank Securities, that there is a 70% chance of a global recession at least as severe as the one in 1973 and 1974.[12]

There are several points to consider when looking at business and the year-2000 problem, each of which most businesses will need to consider.

Risks from Internal Factors

First, there is the question of each company's internal year-2000 preparedness. This includes taking into account all the computerized systems that may have year-2000 vulnerability, especially in the so-called *mission-critical systems*— systems that are absolutely essential to the continued functioning of the business. While it may be important to check other systems, such as security, fire, elevators and the like, a business could probably get around a temporary loss of service. However, if the computer system pertaining to accounts receivable breaks down and the company's cash flow disappears, the company may find itself hard pressed to continue business operations.

So which businesses are at risk? Capers Jones, a leading speaker on software productivity, has estimated that mid-size companies, with between 1,000 and 10,000 employees, are probably at greatest risk as they "historically show a distressing tendency to use quite a lot of software, [but are only] marginally competent in how they build and maintain this software."[13] Jones adds that smaller companies with up to 100 employees may be severely impacted but because they own little software, they can probably manage. In addition, Jones believes that large companies with more than 10,000 employees, while probably greatly impacted by the costs of fixing their year-2000 problems, are generally aware of the problem and have the financial resources available to move towards year-2000 compliance. In all, Jones estimates the probability of failure of the approximately 30,000 mid-size companies to be between five to seven percent—or between 1,500 to 2,100 companies.[14]

Risks from External Factors

Regardless of a company's own year-2000 preparedness, risks from external factors can materially affect its ability to conduct operations. There are several possibilities:

- A company may not be able to obtain materials needed for producing products.
- Apart from materials, a company may not be able to obtain services from third-party contractors because of their lack of year-2000 compliance. Therefore, the company may be unable to follow through on its commitments, potentially harming earnings.
- Customers having year-2000 problems that prevent them from buying the company's services or products can potentially harm earnings.

Companies must follow tax laws in expensing year-2000 costs. Because year-2000 costs can be quite large, they can materially impact the company's revenue or earnings, in turn driving the price of the stock down. In general, we investors don't like it when the value of our investments decrease. More information on this topic will be presented in the next section, specifically regarding a company's responsibility to report potential year-2000 related

Time Out!

The legend of El Dorado came from the custom of the South American Muysca tribe of anointing each new chief with a sticky, resinous gum, then covering him with gold dust. The "shining one" then dove into a sacred lake to wash off while his followers threw emeralds and gold into the water as offerings. Although this custom ceased before the Spanish conquistadors arrived on the shores of the New World, the legend persisted. When the Spanish first heard the tale, they called the chief El Dorado, the golden one. As with many treasure stories, this one grew with the telling, and El Dorado came to mean a city of gold.

Source: Kenneth C. Davis. Dont Know Much About Geography, Avon Books, New York, 1992, p. 117-118.

problems and cost in annual reports to the Securities and Exchange Commission.

There is another very serious concern that could impact businesses—litigation. Some experts estimate that litigation costs associated with year-2000 issues could exceed the cost of fixing year-2000 problems, potentially over a *trillion* dollars. While we have seen only a handful of lawsuits to date, it's likely that the number of lawsuits will increase throughout 1999 and continue through 2000 and beyond. Companies might be sued for at least two reasons.

- Breach of contract, e.g., not being able to deliver promised services or goods that are year-2000 compliant. A case in point is the grocery store that sued the maker of its electronic cash-register system because the system failed every time a customer used a credit card with an expiration date past 1999.
- Class-action lawsuits from shareholders, e.g., the loss of share value when investors weren't properly given information as to how the year-2000 might have impacted the company. This is a touchy issue for many companies. They don't want to make promises they can't keep, such as pledging to fix their year-2000 problem when certain factors may be outside of their control. As a result, some companies are reluctant to talk about potential impact, an action that is equally likely to get them sued if they experience material impact resulting from year-2000 problems.

And what about mergers and acquisitions? Certainly a company that is poorly prepared for the year-2000 would not be attractive to potential buyers. To discover too late a company's high year-2000 risk could be disastrous for the health of the combined company as well as for investors.

The Last Word—Planning Ahead

The year-2000 problem presents uncertainties for investors and businesses alike. And as has been observed many times, the market hates uncertainty, responding with volatility that can shake the composure of even of the most stalwart investors. And it is uncertainty that further causes decisions to be made out of fear—with emotion rather than reason.

In preparation for the year 2000 and to ensure the security of your investments, you must make decisions that are right for you, taking into account your needs, comfort level with risk, and tolerance of volatility. Seeking advice from knowledgeable professionals and observing the year-2000 progress of the markets and businesses will help you plan your own investment strategy for the year 2000.

Timely Tips—Guidelines for the Millennium

So what is an investor to do? With the potential for such a serious impact on the value of stocks, mutual funds, IRAs, 401Ks, and the like, what are your options? Should you view the year-2000 as a problem? Or an opportunity?

Viewing the year 2000 as an opportunity may seem strange to some. Certainly, while the year-2000 problem could have a serious, negative impact on business, from an investment standpoint at least, there is also opportunity. This section will explore actions investors could take to prepare for the year 2000.[15] Prior to making any final decision, it would be wise to consult a professional investment advisor.

Taking Stock

To assess your particular situation, begin by taking stock. Here is a partial list of things to consider:

- What investments do you own? Make a list of stocks, bonds, and mutual funds.
- If you have funds invested in retirement funds, such as IRAs, Keoghs, and 401Ks, you will want to know how they are invested.
- What is your investment process? Do you deal directly with a broker, invest over the Internet, or through a money manager or financial advisor?

Evaluating a Broker, Money Manager, or Financial Advisor

One of the chief complaints people had during recent periods of market instability was the difficulty they encountered, due to communication problems, in trying to reach their broker and their subsequent inability to make trades. Here are some questions from the SEC web site at <www.sec.gov> to ask brokerages, money managers, and investment companies to see how they are preparing for the year 2000:

- What is your firm doing to become year-2000 compliant?
- How can I be satisfied that your firm will be ready on time?
- If your firm is not ready, how could I be affected?
- Will your firm be participating in industry-wide testing?
- What will your firm do for me if I want to sell stock in December 1999 or early January 2000, and my sale is delayed or can't be executed because your firm, or some other market participant, is having computer problems?
- How is your research department evaluating year-2000 compliance of companies before making buy-and-sell recommendations? Is your research department specifically determining if the year-2000 problem could result in a material impact?
- How can I be assured that my interest and dividend payments will not be affected by the year-2000 problem?

Picking a Good Stock

In theory, the metric used in evaluating a company's investment potential while considering the year-2000 computer problem is simple: if a company is not Y2K prepared, their stock could go down. However, this metric is an oversimplification as there are always a number of factors involved in the valuation of stock prices. Here are some factors to consider:

- Is this company more or less at risk for experiencing year-2000 problems? This is an important consideration because the risk is not equal for all companies. The year-2000 risk of a high-tech manufacturing firm is probably greater than that of a company whose operations are decidedly low-tech. In general, businesses that rely more heavily on technology are at greater risk than those that do not. However, as noted before, larger companies also do a better job than mid-size corporations in managing their technology. Because each business is unique, you should carefully examine its year-2000 plans, including policies and contingencies.
- Overseas interests may cause some companies to have greater year-2000 exposure than others. Some banks, for example, providing loans in countries that have not adequately addressed their year-2000 problems may be at greater risk than others banks. In addition, companies importing or exporting goods may be at higher risk if overseas locations can't deliver or receive goods due to their year-2000 problems.

- Overall financial health of a company is important. In the event a company experiences added year-2000 burdens, what is the likelihood the company will be able to address those problems or survive a period with reduced or no revenue? Companies with large cash reserves are probably in a better position to weather any year-2000 related difficulties than a company that is cash strapped.
- Increased risk for litigation as a result of their year-2000 services or products should be considered. This might be more difficult to ascertain, but generally companies dealing in high-technology products, such as software or hardware, may be at increased risk depending on the product.
- Loss of business due to the customers' year-2000 concerns contributes to a company's year-2000 exposure. Consider the following, for example. Company A has a sizable year-2000 problem and devotes more of their budget to fixing the problem. This means company A buys fewer products from Company B than they otherwise would have. As a result, Company B's revenue is down because, overall, it sells fewer products.

Information Sources

Where does an investor get information to make informed decisions? Recently, as a protective measure for investors, the Securities and Exchange Commission (SEC) stipulated that year-2000 specific information be included in annual reports. A tremendous amount of information regarding company financial status can be obtained online via the SEC's Electronic Data Gathering, Analysis, and Retrieval Service (EDGAR). The majority of publicly traded companies are required to make SEC filings electronically, allowing investors to make investment decisions quickly. This site can be reached through the SEC's main home page at <www.sec.gov>

The SEC has become increasingly more active in addressing the year-2000 problem. On July 30, 1998, the SEC updated regulations requiring publicly traded companies to provide year-2000 information to investors. The SEC believed this action was necessary after finding that companies were not providing the information that investors needed, stating, "While the number of companies disclosing Year 2000 issues has increased dramatically, the task force surveys show that many companies are not providing the quality of disclosure that we believe investors expect."[16]

To address this problem, the SEC determined that public companies must disclose year-2000 information if[17]

- its assessment of year-2000 issues is not complete, *or*
- management determines that the consequences of its year-2000 issues would have a material effect on the company's business, results or operations, or financial condition.

In addition, each company's assessment must include whether third parties with whom a company has material relationships are year-2000 compliant. Therefore, if suppliers to a company or customers of a company are likely to experience year-2000 problems, the company must note this in its disclosure.

The SEC has determined that, "in the absence of clear evidence of readiness, a company must assume that it will not be year-2000 compliant and weigh the likely results of this unpreparedness."[18] This is an important determination because it means that companies must assume and anticipate that they will have year-2000 problems unless they have evidence to the contrary. This is good protection for the investor concerned about year-2000 issues.

Because the SEC expects the majority of companies will have year-2000 issues to resolve, businesses must provide additional disclosure information, including:

- The company's state of readiness. The company must describe its year-2000 problems, including difficulties with computer systems and embedded technology systems, in sufficient detail so that investors can understand its year-2000 risks. Additionally, companies must disclose the phase of their reparations and an estimate of how much more time is necessary to achieve completion.
- The costs to address the company's year-2000 issues. The SEC believes that a company must include the costs for modifying its computer systems and hiring year-2000 solutions providers. The company must also provide an estimate of how much more it will need to spend to become compliant.
- The company's contingency plans. "Companies must describe how they are preparing to handle the most reasonably likely worst case scenarios."[19] This will challenge most companies as the majority have yet to devise a contingency plan. In the event no contingency plan exists, the company must state that none exists, as well as when, or if, it will prepare one.

Gathering Information About Investment Opportunities

The following questions from the SEC web site can serve as a guide for ascertaining information about current investments or investment opportunities.

- What is the company doing to prepare its computers for the year 2000?
- What is the anticipated impact of the year-2000 computer problem on the company?
- Is the year-2000 problem for this company primarily internal, operational, or could there be an impact on the company's products and/or services?
- What is the company's schedule for fixing and testing its systems? What progress have they made on this schedule thus far? Can I get a copy of this schedule?

- How will the company's costs in addressing the year-2000 problem affect its earnings? Do these costs have a material financial effect?
- Can I receive a recent company report or other public statement in which the company discusses its approach to the year-2000 problem?
- What are the costs so far and what does the company anticipate it will spend on fixing its year-2000 problems, even if it is not expected to represent a material cost?
- Have any of the company's officers or members of the board bought personal liability insurance specifically for year-2000 problems?
- What is the best assessment of corporate exposure to legal actions arising from equipment or software failures associated with the company's products or services?

Using the Information to Your Advantage

So how do investors use this information to their advantage? Well, some companies are going to be better prepared than their competition. This could potentially allow the better-prepared businesses to increase earnings and market share at their competitors' expense. As a result, shareholder value could potentially increase. In addition, companies that go through significant change as a result of their year-2000 reparations are likely to be leaner and more efficient than before. Again, this could result in increased revenues, market share, and investor value. Of course, as with all investing, some speculation is involved in trying to take advantage of the year-2000 situation.

Identifying a good investment requires a lot of homework and a thorough understanding of the companies and markets involved. The assistance of a professional could pay off if you're interested in pursuing this line of investment.

Mutual Funds

Mutual funds are frequently termed *baskets of stocks*. One of the advantages of mutual funds is that they allow for a broader, more diverse investment portfolio as a result of the pooling of many individual investor funds.

A difficulty facing investors in mutual funds is ascertaining the holdings of any particular fund. Mutual funds can often have holdings in hundreds of companies, and typically buy and sell company stock on a daily basis. Many funds don't want the companies in their portfolios to be public information.

Mutual fund companies, like others, must contend with their own internal and external year-2000 related problems. It behooves an investor in mutual funds to ask questions. Specifically, the SEC has determined that larger investment advisors (with at least $25 million in assets under management

and registered with the SEC) and mutual funds must file report ADV-Y2K.[20]
The SEC had proposed that ADV-Y2K include the following information:[21]
- The scope and status of the advisor's year-2000 compliance plan
- The commitment by the advisor of resources and personnel to address year-2000 issues
- The systems that may be affected by the year-2000 problem
- Progress on six steps, including 1) awareness of potential year-2000 problems, 2) assessment of steps that must be taken, 3) implementation of those steps, 4) internal testing of year-2000 compliant software, 5) testing with service providers, 6) implementation of corrected software
- Contingency plans in the event that the advisor experiences year-2000 difficulties after December 31, 1999
- Readiness of third-party critical systems upon whom the advisor relies

Form ADV-Y2K must be filed twice. The first report must be filed on or before December 7, 1998. The second, an update, must be filed on or before June 7, 1999. In addition, investment companies, including mutual funds, may need to report information to the SEC regarding the year-2000 readiness of the companies in their portfolio, but this issue is not clear at this time.

IRAs and 401Ks

IRAs and 401Ks investments are frequently made in mutual funds and, therefore, face the same year-2000 risks as mutual fund companies. However, there are several additional concerns for these investments.
- Especially with 401Ks, how you invest your retirement funds is limited to the options your employer offers, which is usually a modest choice of investments, ranging from higher risk stock funds to more conservative bonds or U.S.-backed securities. You may wish to encourage the investment services department in your company to offer additional choices.
- A second problem deals with the issue of divestiture. Unfortunately, with tax-deferred investments there is a penalty for early withdrawal as well as a requirement to pay taxes on the receipts. If your are concerned your investment will lose value as the year 2000 approaches, and are thus considering withdrawal of your money from an IRA or 401K, you will want to consider the impact of paying taxes and penalties.

Because of the additional difficulties in preparing for the year 2000 with these forms of investments—as with *all* forms of investment—you should consider talking to a professional who is familiar with your particular situation and who can advise you accordingly.

[1] Readiness of the United States Securities Industry and Public Companies to Meet the Information-Processing Challenges of the Year 2000, Second Report. Securities and Exchange Commission. 1998. Report available from the SEC at <http://www.sec.gov>

[2] Proposed Rule: Investment Adviser Year 2000 Reports, Securities and Exchange Commission. 1998. Available from the SEC at <http://www.sec.gov>

[3] <http://www.nasdaqnews.com/about/gr_adsv.html>

[4] <http://www.nasdaqnews.com/about/factbook/hist97.html#h3>

[5] Narisetti, Raju, Weber, Thomas, and Quick, Rebecca. 1997. How computers calmly handled stock frenzy. *Wall Street Journal*.

[6] <http://www.nasdaqnews.com/about/technology.html>

[7] Hansell, Saul. 1997. Delays, glitches, and unanswered calls, but nothing like 1987. *New York Times*.

[8] Thomas S. Mulligan, Thomas S and E. Scott Reckard, E. Scott. 1997. Volume overload: trade mania tests computers, humans alike. *Los Angeles Times*.

[9] Securities Industry Test Successfully Simulates Year 2000. 1998. SIA Press Release. Available at the SEC web site <http://www.sec.gov>

[10] Diamond, Michael. 1998. Wall Street passes first Y2K test. *USA Today*. Available at <http://www,usatoday.com>

[11] Second Report: Readiness of the United States Securities Industry and Public Companies to Meet the Information-Processing Challenges of the Year 2000, June 1998, Securities and Exchange Commission. Available from the SEC web site at <http://www.sec.gov>

[12] Prepared Testimony of Ed Yardeni, Chief Economist and Managing Director, Deutsche Bank Securities, before the Senate Committee On Agriculture, Nutrition, and Forestry, July 22, 1998, page 2. Available at <http://www.senate.gov/~agriculture/yardeni.htm>

[13] Jones, Capers. 1998. The year 2000 software problem: quantifying the costs and assessing the consequences. *ACM Press*: New York New York page, 168.

[14] *Ibid.*

[15] Seek professional advice. The year-2000 problem is an unknown quantity. Likewise, investing has inherent risks, even when times are good. The information in this book should not be construed as a replacement for qualified, professional advice. Please note that neither the author nor the publisher is engaging in rendering legal or accounting advice. You should always seek the opinion of a licensed broker, CPA, or financial planner who is familiar with your individual circumstances and investment objectives.

[16] Interpretation: Disclosure of Year 2000 Issues and Consequences by Public Companies, Investment Advisers, Investment Companies, and Municipal Securities Issuers, Securities and Exchange Commission, July 29, 1998. Available at <http://www.sec.gov/rules/concept/33-7558.htm>

[17] *Ibid.*

[18] *Ibid.*

[19] *Ibid.*

[20] Investment Advisor Year 2000 Reports, Final Rule, Securities and Exchange Commission. 1998. Available at <http://www.sec.gov/rules/final/ia-1769.htm>

[21] Investment Advisor Year 2000 Reports, Proposed Rule, Securities and Exchange Commission. 1998. Available at <http://www.sec.gov/rules/proposed/ia-1728.htm>

Chapter 7

Telecommunications and the Year 2000

In this chapter you will learn:

- Why telecommunications are vital in today's world
- About year-2000 vulnerabilities in the telecommunications network
- How the Internet works and what must be done to avoid year-2000 problems
- How cell phones could be affected by the year-2000 problem

Living in a Wired World

Imagine the concern you would feel if you couldn't call your family and friends. The frustration if you couldn't reach customer service or airline reservations offices. Or get a medical procedure authorized by your insurance company. Imagine the impact on business and government if orders, important account information, or electronic payments could not be transmitted. What if you needed emergency services but couldn't make the call? Smooth, efficient communication isn't a luxury. It's a necessity.

The need for reliable telecommunications is a concern to all, and the possible consequences of its unavailability has not been lost on people in high places. Senator Bob Bennett made note of his concern in his opening statement on a committee hearing regarding communications:

> . . . the global telecommunications infrastructure is the central nervous system of modern society. Daily, 270 million Americans depend on this complex web of voice, data, and video services that enable their telephones, radios, fax machines, computer networks, televisions and other information appliances. Major national and international enterprises, such as emergency response, national security, finance, transportation, health care, government, energy distribution, and others,

are critically dependent on reliable, 24 hours a day, seven days a week telecommunications.[1]

Because the telecommunications network is perceived as absolutely essential, many people are seriously concerned about the year-2000 progress of the companies involved. The Gartner Group, having researched the progress of various industry sectors, reported that the worldwide telecommunications industry hasn't made much more progress than the worst prepared, such as healthcare, food processing, and government.[2] Telecommunication services are vital, and the challenges facing the industry can potentially affect your ability to communicate with the outside world.

As the way we work continues to evolve, Americans are discovering the benefits of telecommuting, working at home several days per week instead of commuting to the office. Technology such as cell phones, computers, the Internet, fax machines, and email allow people to work away from the office. *Business Week* recently reported that nearly 10 million people are now working outside of their offices at least three days per week.[3] Some employers have widely accepted the practice of telecommuting. At Cisco Systems, for example, 66% of their workforce reportedly telecommutes.[4] And all of this technology depends on the reliable functioning of the telecommunications network. Without it, telecommuting would simply not exist.

This chapter looks at communication services, its vital role in our society, and explores the role of computer systems and potential year-2000 problems. This information should help you determine what contingencies to include as a part of your overall year-2000 strategy.

Time Out!

*A **very** long distance call. Before satellites, before microwave towers, before transatlantic cable, it was a long distance call from New York to London—a very long distance. After four years of experimentation, AT&T and the British Postal Office introduced the first commercial long distance radio-telephone service in 1927. Other countries were added to the network, Canada, Australia, South Africa, Egypt and Kenya—and even ships at sea. This system used fourteen dedicated radio frequencies, with the main transmitter in England. It would be another fifty years before the first transatlantic cable would be laid.*

Source: Telephone History Part 3 Ð 1921 to 1984 by Tom Farley
http://www.privateline.com/TelephoneHistory3/History3.html

Scoping the Problem—One Ringy Dingy

The size of the telecommunications industry is almost beyond belief. The global telecommunications market is worth approximately $670 billion dollars and is expected to increase to about $1 trillion by the year 2000.[5] In terms of call volume, AT&T alone reports handling a daily volume on average of 240 million calls, with about 76 billion calls in the year 1997. In addition, AT&T has placed a network of over 40,000 miles of fiber optic cable throughout the United States, which is part of the reason why every call going through AT&T has 134 possible routes. And that's just AT&T.

The telecommunications network is technologically complex. When making a call, you first dial a number, which is an address that provides information for directing the call. This code is received by a switching device that, as part of its programming, contains information about how to get a call through. This switching device considers the different routes available, selects one, and then sends the data along a trunk line, or pathway, to another switching system. This switching system contains more information on how to find the phone registered to the specific person you are trying to contact and the pathways available to get the call to its destination. After this switching device sends the information through, the phone on the other end rings. There are likely to be several of these network switches working at any one time to connect your call. Each one of these computerized switches must be year-2000 compliant.

FCC Commissioner Michael K. Powell provided a similar, yet more complex explanation:

> . . .in milli-seconds, a phone call from Washington, D.C. to New York travels from your telephone, to the Private Branch Exchange (i.e., switchboard) in your building, to the local exchange carrier's central office switch, through the carrier's network components and systems that route your call to an inter-exchange carrier (or carriers), through long-distance trunk lines (or other telecommunications facilities, like microwave, satellite, fiber-optic), to another local exchange carrier's central switch, and ultimately to the telephone on the other end. Make the same call two minutes later and the call may be routed in a completely different manner as calculated by the network.[6]

Switches are the backbone of the telephone system and are complex machines responsible for opening a connection from one point to another, from my telephone to yours. The earliest network switches were, of course, people. Some of you may remember picking up a phone and asking to be connected to someone, say . . . Bob. The operator knew who Bob was and provided a direct connection from your phone to Bob's phone. Now, switches are highly computerized systems that are capable of handling thousands and even millions of calls at any one time.

These network switching systems also provide crucial business information about your call. When a connection is made, a computer system records the start and end time of your call, as well as the rate per minute. These computers track the year, month, day, hour, minute, and second your call starts and ends. This data is then passed along to a billing computer that keeps track of this information, which is later used to charge you for the call.

This date-related information about your phone call is important. If computers are not year-2000 compliant, people could receive erroneous phone bills. An oft-cited scenario in the popular press is of someone making a call just before midnight, December 31, 1999 and continuing to talk into January, 1, 2000—then being charged for 99 years worth of long-distance calling time!

And there are other computer systems at work, including those that provide services such as call waiting, caller ID, and voice mail. Further, there are computer systems used in the scheduling of repairs as well as for turning service on and off. All of these computers have to work seamlessly to provide the services we have come to rely on.

Can You Hold, Please?

Government agencies as well as businesses—car-rental companies, hospitals, insurance companies, airline reservations, government agencies like Medicare, customer service departments, and so on receive tremendous volumes of calls, most of which are managed by call centers. Like the phone companies, call centers have their own internal networks for handling calls, called private branch exchanges, or PBXs. Like many year-2000 problems, the one facing call centers deals with size. There are simply a huge number of systems and hundreds of millions of lines of computer code to be evaluated and made year-2000 compliant. These PBXs appear to be at risk from year-2000 problems:

Time Out!

Why not 119? The number to call for emergency help is 911. But it hasn't always been so. The first single number for emergency use was 999, used in Great Britain in 1937. During World War II, Yanks stationed in England became familiar with the concept of a central number that would summon law enforcement, fire or ambulance as needed. By the 1950s the U.S. military used a central number for police and fire. But the public had to wait another decade for a single emergency number. Part of the problem was finding a number that was not being used anywhere else as an area code or central office exchange, and that could be easily dialed in the dark. The result of the search—911. The first 911 service was in Haleyville, Alabama in 1968.

Source: Metro-Dade Police Department Website   http://mdpd.metro-date.com/911hist.html

Call centers may not seem to pose a big threat for organizations focused on adapting mainframe applications to handle conversion to the year 2000. But these organizations could be in for a nasty surprise: On Jan 1, 2000, call centers could route customer service calls to the wrong destination, feed inaccurate data to other systems or crash completely.[7]

For information about trading systems, see Chapter 6, *Investment and the Year 2000.*

While call centers may continue receiving phone calls, the computers that provide information—about what to do with the call, what messaging options are available, where to send it, and what to do if the number is busy—might not operate. For you and me, this inconvenience might be just that, an inconvenience. But for businesses that rely on communications, such as brokerage firms and banks, this prospect is terrifying as their operational functions are put at risk.

Replacing non-compliant hardware can be expensive as network switches easily cost tens of thousands of dollars each. And for the system to work, software must be compliant, too. However, call centers don't always upgrade to the most current versions of software. If something works, why change it—especially if upgrading means dealing with complications introduced by undiscovered bugs in the software. As reported in *InformationWeek*, postponing the upgrade to current software versions may be common:

As much as 25% of installed call-center equipment may need to be replaced to handle the year 2000, according to Dataquest Inc., a market research firm in San Jose, Calif. Major switch vendors have been offering year 2000 compliant products since the mid-1990's. But about half of users don't upgrade their technology regularly.[8]

The View from On High

An enormous number of companies offer telecommunications services. In a Senate hearing on the status of the telecommunications industry, Senator Bob Bennett commented:

> Today in the United States, there are five long distance carriers (not including the growing number of long distance resellers), five major national television broadcasters, six Regional Bell Operating Companies, more than one thousand small phone companies, 16 communications satellite providers, more than 4500 hundred Internet Service Providers and hundreds of cellular phone companies, thousands of broadcast radio stations and over eleven thousand cable services companies. And this just captures the infrastructure of the United States and does not include the thousands of large and small communications equipment manufacturers.[9]

The concern with the number of companies involved is twofold. First, because there are so many companies, based simply on the odds, some of them will not have their systems or products year-2000 compliant. If a small local company has non-compliant systems, perhaps in a rural area, the number of customers affected by lack of year-2000 preparedness could be small. However, the larger the company, the greater the potential for communication disruptions for a larger number of people.

Second, the telecommunications system is a network of interdependent providers and equipment manufacturers. Like the proverbial weakest link in the chain, a non-compliant company can cause difficulties even for those companies that are compliant. FCC Commissioner Michael Powell, in a hearing by the Senate Special Committee on the Year 2000 Technology Problem, commented on the year-2000 problem and these interdependencies:

> . . .in order to fix the Year 2000 Problem, the carriers rely on manufacturers of central offices switches and other network equipment. And then there are the end users which must make sure their equipment-such as their telephones, voice mail systems, Private

Branch Exchanges (PBXs), and local area computer networks - are all Year 2000 ready otherwise they will not be able to send or receive voice and data traffic. These groups are, in turn, dependent upon other manufacturers for their equipment, who are in turn, dependent yet again on other providers for parts and services like power. And on it goes.[10]

Cellular Phone Market

Cell phones play an increasingly important role in the daily routine of many people, especially for those whose jobs requires them to be on the go. While business people have been the traditional users in this market, more cell phones are being used for non-business purposes—even the mother driving the car pool is likely to have a cell phone with her. Although smaller than the local and international telecommunications markets, valued at about $500 billion, the cellular market still commands a respectable $28 billion.[11]

Cellular phones are basically small receivers and transmitters. When you call from your cell phone, like a radio station, you are sending a signal that is received by local cellular sites. You have probably seen some of these receivers on the tops of buildings and along highways. The signal is subsequently transmitted through a network of fiber-optic cables that send it on to its destination. If the call is being sent to another cell phone, the signal must be returned to the wireless network, and the transmitter nearest to your current location sends you the message. The system knows where you are because, when your cell phone is on, it sends a signal every so many minutes notifying the network of your location. The cell phone companies are intimately connected with and reliant on all the other components in the telecommunications network. As a result, you cell phone is just as vulnerable to year-2000 problems as the phone on your desk at work or on the wall at home in your kitchen.

1-2-3, Testing, Testing

Interdependence is the name of the game. Each segment of the telecommunications industry is dependent on the others. And this brings us to a crucial point. With so many important players, it is virtually impossible to conduct systems-wide, end-to-end testing to make sure the network is year-2000 compliant.

And there is another difficulty in conducting street-wide testing that is unique to the telecommunications industry. Unlike other industries, such as the financial sector that can test their market systems after they are closed in the evenings and on weekends, the telecommunications network never rests. It is always in service and cannot be disconnected to test the system. Therefore, this industry has to find other means of testing their systems for year-2000 compliance, somehow ensuring that they will work when it all comes together on January 1, 2000.

It's a Small World

Telecommunication services have made the world a much smaller, more intimate place. It is easy in our high-tech society to fax or phone individuals and businesses around the globe. It should come as no surprise, therefore, that there are international telecommunications concerns for the year 2000. Telecommunication companies around the world are interlinked and all face the same millennial challenges. The following concern from Great Britain mirrors concerns here in the United States:

> Telecom users and operators fear a collapse of the global network unless there is an international effort to coordinate millennium bug fixes. . . . Unless it gets suppliers to address the issue immediately, telecom equipment could stop functioning on 1 January [2000]. This could mean we won't be able to make any calls outside the UK.[12]

There are many developing countries, and surprisingly a number of industrialized ones, that either do not have the resources to invest in fixing the problem or have not yet realized the extent of the problem. And some countries, such as those in Southeast Asia and Japan, are facing economic problems that are likely to take precedence over fixing year-2000 problems.[13]

The Internet

Within only a few years, the Internet has become *the next big thing*, with millions of people each year discovering the fascination of the world wide web and the convenience of electronic mail. This rise in popularity is a good example of how rapidly technological advances impact our lives. For some, email is as integral a part of their daily life as is the telephone.

Commerce over the web is expected to grow rapidly as well. Per a report by research firm International Data Corporation (IDC), the highlights of which are available at IDC's website at <www.idc.com>, commerce over the Internet is expected to grow from a few billion dollars in 1998 to more than $400 billion by 2002. Similarly, IDC forecasts that 320 million people will access the Web in 2002, up from the 100 million by the end of 1998.[14]

Although it has ballooned in popularity, not many know how the Internet works. Most of us are only aware that we need to click the mouse a few times before things begin appearing on our screens. But, there are several layers to the Internet—from the applications we interact with, such as a web browser, to the actual physical hardware that controls those millions of bits of information streaming around the globe at the speed of light.

Unlike the phone system, the Internet delivers messages via packets, or packet switching. When you dial a number on the phone, a dedicated connection is created that will stay open for the length of your call—one continuous flow of information. However, information over the Internet is sent in short bursts, or packets of information, with lots of space in between. Because there are long periods of empty space, dedicated, open connections that aren't being used don't make sense. This is where sending packets of information comes into play. Each packet contains the address of its destination, and when these packets reach your computer, they are put back together in the correct order. It only appears that you have a continuous connection on your computer.[15] An excellent article, printed in *American Scientist*, aptly described the difference between the two methods: A circuit-switched network has to find a path for a connection only once, but a packet-switched network has to route every packet individually. It's as if you had to dial a separate telephone call for each word you spoke.[16] These packets are sent via computer systems called routers—expensive machines that continuously send and receive information using the telecommunications infrastructure as its backbone.

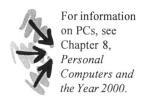 For information on PCs, see Chapter 8, *Personal Computers and the Year 2000.*

The Internet could not exist without the hardware of the telecommunications industry. This physical layer of the Internet that connects us to each other is made up of miles of copper wire and fiber-optic cable. There are other aspects to the Internet which are integral to its operation—*personal computers*, which you are familiar with, and *servers*, computers that store files and make the information available on demand. And each of these systems has its own year-2000 concerns and weaknesses.

Since the Internet is a global network, with packets of information zipping from computer to computer, the impact of a non-compliant computer system is not yet clear. While some argue that there would be little if any impact, others believe that problems could be serious.

The morning of July 17, 1997 was challenging for Internet users. A single, relatively small problem had snowballed into a very large one. The data in a computer responsible for holding domain names was corrupted. A computer holding domain names is like a telephone book—a domain name is an address indicating a web-page location. Imagine the problem you would have if the numbers in your telephone book were incorrect. Other computers gathered information from the computer holding the corrupted data and passed this data along to other computers, which passed the corrupted data on to other computers, and so on. A report in the *New York Times* described the consequences:

> . . . countless thousands or even millions of e-mail messages had been returned as undeliverable, while untold numbers of users had been unable to make contact with various World Wide Web sites whose addresses were temporarily garbled.[17]

Small problems can become big headaches quickly. If this Internet chaos was the result of a small problem, what kind of headache could result from a big problem—like the year-2000 issue?

The Last Word—A Call for Action

Reference has been made throughout this book to the problem of interdependency. Perhaps no other industry exemplifies this better than the telecommunications industry. The many layers of equipment manufacturers and service providers make for a complicated system that will require enormous effort and expense in order to minimize year-2000 problems. And while much of this is outside the ability of any individual to circumvent, there are still things that can be done to minimize any year-2000 risks.

Timely Tips—Guidelines for the Millennium

Because of the complexities and cost involved in developing telecommunications networks, there are few ways for the average person to develop workable alternatives. However, there are several actions you can take to deal with potential year-2000 telecommunications problems.

What are Your Telecommunications Uses and Needs?

To ascertain the degree of impact from a potential loss of reliable telecommunications, first determine your telecommunication uses and needs. Ask yourself the following questions to get an idea as to your telecommunications risk areas:

- How important are reliable telecommunications to and from your home? Do you use the phone primarily for calling friends, scheduling appointments and the like? Do you pay bills over the Internet?
- Is there anyone at your home that is more likely to be at risk without reliable telecommunications during the transition into the year 2000? Elderly parents, young children, or an expectant mother, for example.
- What are your business needs for telecommunications services? Scheduling appointments, contacting customers, ordering materials, and talking with the home office, are examples.
- Has your company assessed its PBX system (if it has one) for year-2000 problems to determine if calls will be able to come in and get out?
- How do you use telecommunications services to conduct business? Do you use the phone on business travel? Do you check for messages and appointments using your cell phone? Do you fax information and estimates to customers?
- Are your business communications primarily local, within the United States, or international?
- How important is it to stay in close contact with overseas business associates and customers?
- How much business do you conduct over the Internet or a company intranet?
- What contingency plans has your business developed to deal with the potential loss of communications with important customers, customer service, employees, and business contacts?

Loss of Telecommunications Service

For most people, a loss of telecommunication service to their homes for a few days will be more of an inconvenience than a serious concern. If a telecommunications blackout occurred for a long period of time, however, it might make it difficult to schedule appointments, talk to family, and so on.

It would be more serious still if there were special considerations at home, such as sick children or parents with health problems. The loss of telecommunications would eliminate the ability to dial 911 in emergencies.

The loss of telecommunications would probably impact business operations almost immediately. A tremendous amount of business is conducted via the telecommunications network—phones, faxes, voice mail, email, e-commerce, customer service, toll-free numbers for ordering products, and the like. The loss of these services, even for a short period of time, would have a serious negative impact. And the effect would be compounded if your business needs require international travel or communication with overseas clients or customers.

Tips for Overseas Telecommunications

The reliability of overseas telecommunications in the year 2000 is an open question. Unfortunately, many countries simply are not well prepared to deal with the year-2000 problem and the potential ramifications, increasing the likelihood of problem areas.

If you travel or call overseas frequently, you may want to try to conduct as much business as possible before the turn of the century rather than after. It may be wise to develop contingency plans in the event you lose communications for a period of time, anticipating problems and devising solutions ahead of time. This will help minimize problems and leave you feeling less anxious in the event communications are down.

Long Distance Options

The cost to develop your own long-distance telecommunications network is obviously prohibitive. This leaves you at the mercy of the telecommunications carriers and equipment manufacturers, and the effectiveness of their year-2000 plans.

However, there may be some actions you can take. The major carriers, such as AT&T and Sprint, each own their own communications network, although they must obviously connect with each other at some cross-over point. Because there are several networks, including wireless networks as well as cable, there is a redundancy built into the system that you may be able to take advantage of—that is, if there are only sporadic outages and not a global meltdown in telecommunications service.

To take advantage of this redundancy you need to be able to access their network, either by dialing a series of digits prior to making a call or by dialing an 800 number and using your account code. One thing to keep in mind is that many smaller telecommunications companies buy long-distance time from the larger carriers, so you may or may not actually be accessing a separate network. Ask if the carrier has their own network or from whom they buy time so you don't inadvertently duplicate your access to the same major carrier.

In some limited cases it may be possible to use your cell phone even though standard phone services are inoperative. Although it would be unwise to rely on this alternative, it is worth a try.

Other Telecommunications Options

In the event you lose telecommunications services, there may be some other options for communication with the outside world.

- You may want to setup your own small telecommunications system by obtaining a CB radio and setting up a network with friends with whom you can communicate during emergency situations. Don't forget a backup power supply for your CB.
- You may want to get your short-wave radio license, although this could involve significant time and expense. Contact the American Radio Relay League for more information regarding short-wave radio at <www.aarl.org>
- Ham radio operators have often been the backbone of communications in emergency situations. Find out if someone in your neighborhood has short-wave radio equipment.
- For individuals with health or other problems, set up a monitoring system with neighbors.

Dealing with Potential Telecommunications Billing Issues

- If billing computers are not fixed in time, you could receive a *nonsense* phone bill. To minimize this possibility, avoid making phone calls that extend from the evening of December 31, 1999 into January 1, 2000.
- Make copies of your account records in the odd event that your records are lost or otherwise corrupted.

- Contact your company immediately if you do receive a bill showing erroneous delinquent payments. Having copies of your records to show a history of payment could be valuable in this event. If you need to submit copies of your records as proof of payment, keep your originals.

---

[1] Opening Statement of Senator Bob Bennett, Chairman, Special Senate Committee on the Year 2000 Technology Problem, Hearing: Communications of the Challenge of the Year 2000. 1998. Available at <http://www.senate.gov/~bennett/pr073198.html>

[2] Marcoccio, Lou. 1998. Year 2000 world status 2Q98 update - A Summary Report. Gartner Group.

[3] Baig, Edward C. 1998. Saying adios to the office. *Business Week*, Personal Business Section. Edited by Amy Dunkin.

[4] Tergesen, Anne. 1998. Making stay-at-homes feel welcome. *Business Week*, Personal Business section.

[5] Cimino, Daniela. 1997. MCI's change management challenge. *Software Magazine.* October Y2K Special. Available at <http://www.softwaremag.com/Y2K/Y2Koct97/sm1075r1.htm>

[6] Statement of FCC Commissioner Michael K. Powell before the Senate Special Committee on the Year 2000 Problem. 1998. Available at <http://www.fcc.gov.Speeches/Powell/Statements/stmkp819.html>

[7] Thyfault, Mary E. 1997. Call center crisis - outdated PBXs called vulnerable to date-field problems. *Information Week.* Available at <http://www.techweb.com/se/directlink.cgi?IWK19970602S0065>

[8] *Ibid.*

[9] Opening Statement of Senator Bob Bennett, Chairman, Special Senate Committee on the Year 2000 Technology Problem, Hearing: Communicating the Challenge of the Year 2000. 1998.

[10] Statement of FCC Commissioner Michael K. Powell Before the Senate Special Committee on the Year 2000 Problem. 1998. Available at <http://www.fcc.gov.Speeches/Powell/Statements/stmkp819.html>

[11] Elstrom, Peter and Kerwin, Kathleen. 1998. New boss new plan. *Business Week.*

[12] Kennedy, Siobhan. 1997. Phone firms hung up over millennium. *Computer Weekly.*

[13] Statement of FCC Commissioner Michael K. Powell Before the Senate Special Committee on the Year 2000 Problem. 1998. Available at <http://www.fcc.gov.Speeches/Powell/Statements/stmkp819.html>

[14] IDC's Internet Commerce Market Model Predicts Buyers on the Web Will Increase Nearly Tenfold by 2002. Available at <http://www.IDC.com>

[15] Hayes, Brian. 1997. The infrastructure of the information infrastructure. *American Scientist.* Available at <http://www.amsci.org/amsci/Issues/Comsci97/compsci9705.html>

[16] *Ibid.*

[17] John Markoff, John. 1997. Minor error throws Internet into disarray. *New York Times on the Web.* Available at <http://www.nyt.com>

Chapter 8

Personal Computers and the Year 2000

In this chapter you will learn:

- A method for assessing year-2000 bugs in your computer system
- How hardware and software can introduce year-2000 problems
- Options for renovating non-compliant hardware and software

It's an Infestation

With all the emphasis on fixing year-2000 computer problems in the government and large companies, it shouldn't come as a surprise that many of you may have your own year-2000 problem sitting on your desk. Nearly half of all American households contain one or more PCs. And there are millions of small- and home-office computer users. Just because your PC is housed in a small, perhaps cozy, environment doesn't mean it's not affected. The year-2000 problem is a pervasive one, and it is going to take more than a dousing of your favorite bug spray to eliminate the problems. But there are steps you can take to get the problems under control before they start to control you.

Scoping the Problem—A Pesky Little Bug

It appears that many home-business and small-business people are not addressing the year-2000 bug, perceiving the problem, according to one report, to be "little more than a blip."[1] This same study reported that 40% of small businesses have no plans to address possible computer problems.[2] To do nothing, in this case, may not the best answer. This date-related bug could cause you some serious heartburn.

Just what kinds of year-2000 problems might the typical computer user, including small- and home-business users, encounter? It depends on the applications and programs that you use.

- Word processing: automatic date functions in word processing programs may become affected, causing incorrect dates to appear on documents.
- Spreadsheets: two-digit century information may lead to incorrect values being calculated.
- Email: typical sorting by date order could be affected causing messages to be filed at the top of a list instead of at the bottom where new email is usually placed—causing new messages to be overlooked.
- Financial management: some programs may not allow year-2000 entries.
- Automatic archiving: some programs may not backup important work.
- Inventory management: some programs may not provide accurate inventory statistics.

Who's Most at Risk?

Personal computer users are as diverse as the tasks they require of their PCs. Some users whose lives are filled with constant computerized activity are called *power users*. These users tend to want or need the speediest, newest, and costliest computer systems.

For information on the Internet, see Chapter 7, *Telecommunications and the Year 2000*.

At the other end of the spectrum are the *occasional* users who use a personal computer to write a letter periodically. Occasional users tend to buy—and upgrade—according to their need, holding off upgrading to the latest hardware and software for years because they are satisfied with what they have.

The rest of us fall somewhere in the middle—those who frequently use word-processing programs to write letters, finance programs to keep track of our checking and savings accounts, and the Internet to search for information, order a book, or make a plane reservation. And, in all likelihood, we use our computers to play an occasional game or two.

Because the majority of PC users rely on Intel-based computers, using Microsoft's Windows operating system, or Apple Macintosh computers, using the Macintosh operating system (Mac OS), this chapter will discuss only these two computer platforms.

Approaching the Problem

Government agencies and businesses apply a structured approach in order to thoroughly determine the extent of their year-2000 problems. There is good reason for you to do so as well, as a process will help you identify and carefully deal with any year-2000 problems you may find. While there are many approaches, they all involve several basic steps: 1) taking an inventory, 2) assessing the compliance of the items on your inventory, 3) making necessary changes via renovation, and 4) testing the changes to make sure they remain year-2000 compliant.

Step One—Inventory

Before you can do anything, you have to know what might have a year-2000 bug. Therefore, the inventory step involves the listing of your computer system(s) and applications. If you are networked to other computers, as a small business might be, you will want to inventory your networking hardware as well.

Step Two—Assessment

The assessment phase involves determining the compliance of the items on your inventory list—the computer hardware, applications, and any networking equipment. Unfortunately, there is no simple way to know whether your computer system is year-2000 compliant. One clear guideline, however, has to do with the age of your computer system—the older the hardware, operating system, and applications, the greater the likelihood that you may have a year-2000 bug. To determine if you have your own year-2000 problem, you will need to explore where date-related errors might occur—in both the hardware and software.

Hardware Problem Areas

- Internal Clocks: Most computers have internal clocks. These clocks keep time during those periods when power to your computer is turned off or is unavailable, such as during a power outage. Some people may have found that their computer at some point began giving them a strange, non-current date—the first clue that they needed a new internal battery for this clock. This clock is sometimes referred to as a hardware clock or RTC (real-time clock).
- BIOS: Another culprit is something called the BIOS, which stands for Basic Input/Output System. For our purposes, it doesn't really matter that we have a technical understanding of what the BIOS does. It is

important to know, however, that the BIOS checks with the RTC for the current date and time. The BIOS also passes this information on to the operating system. The BIOS itself is not the cause of year-2000 non-compliance. However, the BIOS is part of the problem because it may not be able to recognize incorrect dates and, as a result, allow incorrect dates to be passed on to the operating system and software applications.

In general, the older your hardware the more likely you could have a year-2000 problem. This is certainly the case for the RTC and the BIOS. Greenwich Mean Time, a company which conducted research in this area, found some rather alarming statistics—the majority of BIOSs in personal computers tested failed in some way:[3]

- 93% of BIOSs in computers manufactured prior to 1997 did not rollover successfully to 2000.
- 47% of BIOSs created in 1997 did not rollover successfully to 2000.

Assessing Your Hardware

There is a particular group of individuals for whom the question of hardware year-2000 compliance is not at issue. Macintosh users will be glad to learn that all Macintosh computers, since the very first, have been built with compliant RTCs and BIOSs. However, Mac users may still experience software difficulties with the year-2000 problem, so read the information in the software section.

Before conducting any test, always make sure you have important files backed up in order to safeguard them. In addition, it is wise to make sure that no applications are running, such as word processors or spreadsheets. Don't change your clock settings unless you are certain that the change will not adversely affect your important applications or data. Some shareware, beta programs, and even operating systems are date sensitive because they are programmed to no longer work after a period of time or are licensed to expire after a period of time. Please be aware that changing dates on your computer may cause these programs to become inoperative.

If you don't know if this applies to you or not, you may not want to perform the following tests yourself. Instead, you may prefer to purchase a commercial product that will help you determine the year-2000 status of your hardware. A number of products are now appearing on store shelves that will allow you, for a modest cost, to assess your equipment and even apply a fix if necessary. There are also a number of freeware products available for download on the Internet. But please note, not all software is created equal. It is up to you to determine the reputability of products downloaded over the Internet.

For those interested in conducting their own year-2000 assessment, there are several straightforward tests you can try. These tests are common and have been reported in many magazine and newspaper articles. The first one, referred to as the *odometer test*, checks to see if your computer has the capacity to rollover to a year-2000 date.[4] The second one, which we will call the *continuity test,* verifies that your system can maintain the change after you have turned it off.

There are at least two different ways of performing the Odometer Test and the Continuity Test, via the BIOS setup and through the operating system control panel. In general, it is probably better to conduct the tests via the BIOS setup screen, as any incorrect date information you enter is not passed on to the operating system, applications, and your data.

Year-2000 Odometer Test—Will Your Computer Date Change When it Should?

BIOS Setup Screen:
1. Enter your computer's BIOS setup screen. This is usually done by pressing a key or keys at a specific point during the booting up of your computer. You will need to refer to your computer's documentation to determine this information.
2. Set the date to 12-31-1999.
3. Set the time to 11:58:00 p.m. (23:58 for those using a 24-hour clock).
4. Shut down the computer.
5. Wait for at least two minutes.
6. Turn on your computer and re-enter the BIOS setup screen.
7. If the year does not read 2000, then your system is not year-2000 compliant.
8. Remember to reset your system to the correct date before continuing.

Operating System Control Panel:
1. Go to the control panel.
2. Click on the Date/Time Icon.

3. Set the date to 12-31-1999.
4. Set the time to 11:58:00 p.m.
5. Close the control panel and shut down the computer.
6. Wait for at least two minutes.
7. Turn on your computer and check the date and time.
8. If the year does not read 2000, then your system is not year-2000 compliant.
9. Remember to reset your system to the correct date before continuing.

Your computer's date and time should read 01-01-2000. If it reads some other date, such as January 4, 1980, a date frequently on non-compliant systems, then your system has the year-2000 bug. If your computer says 01-01-00, you don't know if the system thinks it is 2000 or 1900. You may need to set the date/time control panel to display four-digit century dates. Refer to your users manual to make this change if necessary.

Year-2000 Continuity Test—Will Your Computer's Date Stay Accurate?

BIOS Setup Screen:
1. Enter your computer's BIOS setup screen using the same method as you did for the Odometer test.
2. Set your computer's date to 01-01-2000.
3. Turn off your computer.
4. After waiting at least several minutes, turn your computer back on.
5. Enter your computer's BIOS setup screen and look at the date.
6. If the date is other than 01-01-2000 then your computer system failed the Continuance test.
7. Remember to reset your system to the correct date before continuing.

Operating System Control Panel:
1. In the control panel, click on the Date/Time Icon.
2. Set your computer's date to 01-01-2000.
3. Turn off your computer.
4. After waiting at least several minutes, turn your computer back on.
5. Check the date and time. If the date is not 01-01-2000 then your computer did not pass the continuance test.
6. Remember to reset your system to the correct date before continuing.

If compliant, your computer will still read 01-01-2000. If it reads some other date, it is not year-2000 compliant.

Finally, before pronouncing your system complaint or non-compliant, you may want to conduct these tests again, just to be on the safe side.

Assessing Your Software

Software can also present its own year-2000 problems. Regardless of the compliance of the hardware, software has the potential for promoting year-2000 problems throughout your computer. For our purposes, we will examine two categories of software: operating systems and applications.

Operating Systems: The most common operating systems for the consumer are Microsoft's Windows and Apple's Mac OS, so coverage in this chapter will focus on these two systems.

The operating system made by Apple for the Macintosh is and has always been year-2000 compliant. However, software applications, covered in the next section, may not be. Therefore, Mac users could still experience year-2000 problems.

Microsoft, too, claims that its operating systems are compliant, but adds that a number are compliant *with minor issues* (see chart that follows). You may want to check out Microsoft's web site to make sure you don't need to download a file or two. Although compliant in that these operating systems will not produce errors processing date data in connection with the transition to the year 2000, DOS, Windows 3.x, and Windows 95 aren't aware of when they are given an incorrect date from the BIOS. These operating systems will simply use whatever date they are given. This means incorrect dates could be passed along to your applications and data.

Windows 98, however, is date savvy and will recognize if the date from the BIOS is incorrect. In this instance, Windows 98 will apply a correction and pass the corrected date on. Be aware, however, that Windows 98 is *not* fixing the RTC or BIOS. Therefore, any applications bypassing the operating system, going directly to the BIOS or RTC instead, will be using the incorrect date.

Microsoft Windows Year-2000 Compliance

Windows 95 v. 4.00.950	Compliant with minor issues*
Windows 95 (OSR) OEM Services Releases 1, 2, 2.1, 2.5	Compliant with minor issues*
Windows 98	Compliant*
Windows 3.1	Compliant with minor issues*
Windows 3.11	Compliant with minor issues*
Windows for Workgroups 3.11	Compliant with minor issues*

* Microsoft refers users to see specific product compliance documents at their web site for applicable prerequisites.

Source: http://www.microsoft.com//technet/topics/year2k/product/product.htm

Applications: Applications, such as your spreadsheet and financial management program, can also have year-2000 problems. Primarily, incorrect year-2000 dates may occur when applications don't obtain date information from the operating system. Some application programs have their own method of calculating date information, independent of the OS, which may not be year-2000 compliant.

Time Out!

Ever wonder who wrote the first computer program? Born in 1815, August Ada Byron, daughter of the famous poet, Lord Byron, was raised by her mother to be mathematician and scientist. Although Ada married the Earl of Lovelace and became the mother of three children, still she continued to pursue her love of mathematics. At a dinner party she was introduced to the ideas of Charles Babbage for a new calculating engine. Fascinated by his ideas, she became an avid supporter of Babbage and believed that his Analytical Engine might someday be used to compose music, produce graphics, as well as perform mathematical calculations. In her correspondence with Babbage, Ada wrote a plan for how his engine might calculate Bernoulli numbers.

History has borne out Lady Lovelace's fanciful predictions. Although his engine was mechanical in nature, historians credit Babbage with building the first computer, and Ada Lovelace's mathematical plan as the first computer program. And of course, computers do produce graphics, compose music, and perform mathematical calculations—with the help of a good computer programmer.

Source: http://www.cs.yale.edu/homes/Files/ada-bio.html

Examples of potential problems:

- Old Software: Not everybody uses the most recent versions of software. In fact, many are content to continue using programs that are several years old because the programs satisfy their needs—plus the users have grown comfortable with them. But these programs may not calculate year-2000 dates correctly.
- Non-compliant application software: One individual reported trying to enter year-2000 dates in a popular financial management program on a Macintosh—noted to have year-2000 compliant hardware and operating system. To this individual's surprise, he received an error message and found his date entries changed to 1999.[5]

Determining Software Compliance

A simple method of determining compliance of your application programs is to contact the manufacturer, the easiest way being via the Internet. Most software companies will have product year-2000 compliance information listed on their web pages.

Or, if you are overwhelmed by the number of applications on your computer's hard drive or don't want to go searching across the Web, you may purchase a program to help you identify non-compliant programs There are a number of commercial products available that will help you assess your applications (see Tips section). These programs usually compare the applications on your hardware to a database of compliant or non-compliant software applications. Some programs will even offer instructions as to what your options might be if a non-compliant program is discovered.

Step Three—Renovation

The renovation phase involves determining the actions you want to take with equipment or software that is not year-2000 compliant. Options could include doing nothing, upgrading software, or even replacing the hardware altogether.

Renovation of Hardware: What do you do if your system does not pass either or both of the tests? First of all, don't panic—you have some options. If your computer failed test #1, the odometer or rollover test, but passed test #2, the continuity test, you are fortunate. First celebrate the New Year, and second, re-set your computer to the correct date on the morning of January 1, 2000. That's it!

However, if your system failed both tests or the second test alone, you may have to go farther before reaching year-2000 compliance. Following are several options.

- One option depends on whether your BIOS can be upgraded. Some BIOSs can be flash upgraded, or *flashed* for short. Whether or not your particular BIOS can be flashed can usually be determined by checking your user manual or contacting the manufacturer of your computer system by phone or web site. If your BIOS can be flashed, closely follow the instructions provided by the manufacturer.
- If your BIOS cannot be flashed, another option may be to replace the BIOS. However, depending on the manufacturer of your computer and its age, this may not be a good alternative. Replacing a BIOS in a computer is not a job for the typical user as it requires a high level of expertise and confidence. In these instances, call several local computer shops to find out if they can perform the work and what it will cost.
- Finally, there are some software options that may provide a fix for non-compliant hardware. Some companies are selling software packages that intercept the incorrect date from the non-compliant BIOS and RTC, change it to a year-2000 date, then pass it along to the operating system and other applications. In general, this should work unless some of your applications go directly to the RTC for this information, in which case it would still be using an incorrect date. There is no easy way other than by contacting the manufacturer of the software to determine where the application obtains date information.

Renovation of Software: Most people own off-the-shelf programs written by established companies, so determining compliance will generally not be too difficult. Many companies will offer a fix, although some may require you to purchase an upgrade. However, don't be surprised to find that some companies are no longer in business. The software business, as with high technology business in general, is highly competitive, and many companies simply do not survive. In this case, your options are limited. You may have to purchase new software.

Step Four—Testing Your Changes

Essentially, testing involves determining if your changes resulted in a year-2000 compliant system. This involves, at a minimum, conducting the Odometer and Continuity Tests mentioned earlier in the chapter. If not compliant, you will want to repeat the following steps again.

- Inventory: Re-examine your inventory to see if there was something that was missed.
- Assessment: Again, assess your hardware and software to determine if something was overlooked, or if something initially appeared compliant, but wasn't. There have been reports of equipment or software passing an initial test only to fail a second trial.
- Renovations: Renovate any non-compliant hardware or software that was discovered in the previous step.
- Test: Re-test, in order to insure compliance of your system.

The Last Word—To Fix or Not to Fix. That is the Question.

You may find that you have a year-2000 bug of your own. Whether you decide to address the problem, of course, is up to you. The answer depends on your use of computer technology, the cost to fix the problem, and how important addressing the problem is to you. Many small- and home- business owners will find it imperative to fix problems—business may depend on it. Others will want to fix the problem because they can't bear to think of their systems as . . . *buggy*, even if the year-2000 problems they have may not impact their use of the computer very much.

Still, it is impossible to anticipate precisely how the year-2000 problem could affect your computer system, including your important data. And you certainly would not want to pass on bad data to other computer systems. It may be wise, therefore, to err on the conservative side and address as many year-2000 problems as you can.

Timely Tips—Guidelines for the Millennium

A comprehensive list is beyond the scope of this book, but this section contains phone numbers and web addresses for a number of different companies you may want to contact to determine the year-2000 compliance of your hardware or software, or to read a company's year-2000 compliance statement.

Hardware Companies

Acer Group
www.acer.com
www.acer.com/year2000

Hewlett-Packard
www.hp.com
www.hp.com/year2000

IBM
www.ibm.com
www.ibm.com/IBM/year2000

Apple Computer
www.apple.com
www.apple.com/macos/info/2000.html

Intel
www.intel.com
support.intel.com/support/year2000/index.htm

AST Research (Samsung)
www.ast.com
www.ast.com/services/y2k/main.html

Packard-Bell
www.packardbell.com
support.packardbell.com/year2000

Compaq Computer
www.compaq.com
www.compaq.com/year2000/

Toshiba
www.toshiba.com
http://www.csd.toshiba.com/cgi-
bin/WebObjects/Home.woa/-
/WP.wo?TID=41&OID=0

Dell Computer
www.dell.com
www.dell.com/year2000

Gateway
www.gateway.com
www.gateway.com/frameset2.asp?s=corp&p=support&a=&url=/corp/y2k/y2k/default.html

Software Companies

Adobe Systems
www.adobe.com
www.adobe.com/newsfeatures/year2000/main.html
Adobe's Year 2000 information line at 408-536-3500.

Lotus
www.lotus.com
www.lotus.com/home.nsf/tabs/y2k

Corel
www.corel.com
www.corel.com/International/Uk_Ireland/clp/2000.htm

IBM
www.ibm.com
www.ibm.com/IBM/year2000

Microsoft
www.microsoft.com
www.microsoft.com/technet/topics/year2k/default.htm

Intuit
www.intuit.com
www.intuit.com/support/year2000.html

Netscape
www.netscape.com/netscape/index.html
www.netscape.com/products/year2000/faq/client.html

Symantec
www.symantec.com
www.symantec.com/y2k/y2k.html

Software To Identify or Address Year-2000 Problems[6]

To help identify or fix year-2000 problems, you may want to consider a free year-2000 utility before purchasing a package. If you choose this route, make sure the product is from a reputable source. The major computer magazines are great resources for helping find these products and may have conducted testing to determine the pros and cons of each. Some of these magazine may even have a free year-2000 utility you can download directly from their web site.

Computer Magazines

www.pcmag.com
www.winmag.com

Products Claiming to Detect Year-2000 Problems

The following is only a partial listing of the products available. Remember to do your homework on these products before using them. As we get closer to the year 2000 there are likely to be many more applications packages that will aid you in detecting year-2000 problems.

McAfee 2000 toolbox
Network Associates
(www.nai.com)

Nuts & Bolts 98 Deluxe
Network Associates
(www.nai.com)

Check 2000 PC
Greenwich Mean Time
(www.gmt-uta.com)

Norton 2000
Symantec Corporation
(www.symantec.com)

---

[1] Ho, Rodney. 1998. Many small-business owners shrug at year 2000 problem. *The Wall Street Journal*, Interactive Edition. Available at <http://www.wjs.com>

[2] *Ibid.*

[3] Greenwich Mean Time. < http://www.gmt-2000.com/hardware-problem.htm>

[4] Celko, Joe and Celko, Jackie. 1997. Double Zero. *Byte*.

[5] de Jager, Peter. 1997. Year 2000: walking on thin ice. *Datamation*. Available at <http://www.datamation.com/PlugIn/issues/1997/april/04col60.html>

[6] Neither the author or the publisher is making a recommendation or claim as to the reliability of any software mentioned in this book. The information is provided for informational purposes only. You should conduct your own analysis and determine the benefits or consequences of using such products.

Chapter 9

Transportation and Travel and the Year 2000

In this chapter you will learn:

- How computers are used throughout the travel industry
- How the year-2000 problem could impact travel throughout the United States
- How highways, traffic lights, and public transportation could be affected
- What the real year-2000 risk is to elevators
- Why travel outside the United States may not be safe

Planes, Trains, and Automobiles . . . and Subways, Buses, and Ferries

Ours is a mobile society. We depend on transportation to get to work, the grocery store, the doctor's office; to take the children to and from school and then to ballet or soccer practice, and on and on. And most of us take an annual vacation within the U.S. or travel to exotic ports. While many of us depend on the various means of transportation—such as planes, trains and automobiles—for our transportation, millions also rely on buses, subway systems, and even ferries for their daily transportation needs.

It was very different not too long ago. The availability of fast, convenient transportation didn't exist earlier in this century. I remember my grandmother, who grew up in rural Oklahoma, recalling the time she rode in her first automobile—and her surprise at finding the driver had a six-shooter lying on the seat next to him. Come to think of it, maybe some things haven't changed so much! But in all seriousness, it was a simpler time then, with few streets, fewer traffic lights, and certainly no intelligent traffic light management systems.

The fact is, as a society we have become dependent upon transportation. Likewise, our methods of transportation are dependent upon technologies, many of which are date-dependent and at risk for potential year-2000 problems.

Scoping the Problem—An Issue of Titanic Proportion?

Today, most, if not all, modes of transportation are dependent in some way upon automated computerized technologies. While each kind of transportation is unique, they all have in common a reliance on myriad automated processes—many of which are heavily date-dependent. Airplanes, trains, subways, and buses, for example, are heavily dependent upon automated technologies for many functions, from reservations, ticketing, scheduling, and routing to maintenance scheduling and parts inventory.

But while the year-2000 problem could have a serious impact on our ability to get around conveniently, we face an added complication come the turn of the century—the holidays. The year 2000 will arrive during one of the most heavily traveled times of the year. And with the great number of celebrations planned in observance of the new millennium, not just in the United States but around the world, record numbers of revelers could find themselves facing a different kind of headache than they expected on the morning of January 1, 2000.

This chapter is about transportation and travel. Specifically, *people* transportation and travel, versus cargo and product transportation which is covered in *Chapter 10 - Delivery of Goods in the Year 2000*. The twentieth century has been remarkable for many things, including an enormous increase in the type, complexity, and dependency upon transportation systems for our daily needs. And remarkably, many may find themselves walking into the next century.

Aviation

The aviation industry is a multibillion dollar enterprise with thousands of dedicated people working to insure its smooth operation. The industry encompasses a vast array of different, yet interconnected services, from airplane manufacture to ticketing and reservation—all of which take advantage of automated and other computerized technologies to function. As such, the potential for gridlock within the aviation industry because of year-2000 problems is serious. For example, problems at an air-traffic control tower causing ground delays at one airport could have an effect on traffic at other airports across the country and around the world. This domino effect could magnify the problem. One report indicated that six or seven such problems spread in just the right locations could result in gridlock around the globe within just a few days.[1] This section will explore the aviation industry with respect to year-2000 considerations, specifically plane safety, reservations, and ticketing, areas of concern for the typical traveler.

Plane Safety: A number of travelers have voiced concern regarding the effect of the year-2000 problem on the safety of airplanes, recognizing that there are many computerized systems that automate procedures and provide important flight information to the pilots and crew.

While it is true there are hundreds, even thousands of computerized and embedded technologies in use in the modern-day airplane, there appear to be no year-2000 problems that compromise flight safety. According to Boeing, its commercial airplane fleet has been surveyed, including the many suppliers providing parts and systems for their planes, and the only year-2000 concerns identified were nuisance flight deck effects—minor issues not affecting flight or safety—for which upgrade programs are in place.[2] Likewise, Airbus Industrie is confident that, while there are a few minor year-2000 glitches on each plane, none compromise safety.[3]

While this is good news, there is a small caveat. After taking possession of the planes from the manufacturer, airlines may have added equipment that may or may not be year-2000 compliant. Some of this equipment may work with systems important to flight operations. Airlines have been advised to contact these suppliers for information regarding year-2000 compliance. For their part, airlines appear to be actively pursuing this issue.

Federal Aviation Administration: The Federal Aviation Administration (FAA) and its computers play an integral role in air travel safety. The FAA is responsible for many important systems used in managing the thousands of daily domestic flights:

> Integral to executing each of FAA's programs are extensive information processing and communications technologies. For example, each of FAA's 20 en route air traffic control facilities, which controls aircraft at the higher altitudes between airports, depends on about 50 interrelated computer systems to safely guide and direct aircraft. Similarly, each of FAA's almost 100 flight standards offices, responsible for inspecting and certifying various sectors of the aviation industry (e.g. commercial aircraft, repair stations, mechanics, pilot training schools, maintenance schools, pilots, and general aviation

aircraft), are supported by over 30 mission-related safety database and analysis systems. Because of the complexity of the systems supporting FAA's mission, most of these systems are unique to FAA and not off-the-shelf systems that can be easily maintained by system vendors.[4]

Many aviation businesses and agencies are concerned about the interdependencies of their systems with those of the FAA. Representatives of the airlines, aircraft manufacturers, airports, fuel suppliers, telecommunications providers, and industry associations have raised concerns that their own year-2000 compliance work would be irrelevant if the FAA doesn't make their systems compliant in time.[5]

FAA also has numerous, complex information processing interactions with various external organizations, including airlines, aircraft manufacturers, general aviation pilots, and other government agencies, such as the National Weather Service (NWS) and the Department of Defense. Over the years, these organizations and FAA have built vast networks of interrelated systems. For example, airlines' flight planning systems are linked to FAA's Enhanced Traffic Management System, which monitors flight plans nationwide, controls high traffic situations, and alerts airlines and airports to bring in more staff when there is extra traffic. As another example, FAA facilities rely on weather information from NWS ground sensors, radar, and satellites to control and route aircraft.[6]

Of the many systems used by the FAA, air traffic control computers, which track and communicate with flights, have received considerable attention. These computers were made by IBM in the early 1980s, which by industry standards makes them very old. So old in fact, that IBM recommended that the FAA retire these systems as neither the parts nor people with the skills needed to conduct repairs are available.[7]

However, at the time of this writing, the FAA had declined to replace these computers, deciding to find solutions to fix these systems. One problem the FAA has already discovered involved a command enabling a computer to switch from one cooling pump to another. If not fixed, the computer could have overheated, leading to a potential computer failure.[8]

Several other of the FAA's critical systems have been found to have year-2000 problems:[9]

- Systems used in the En-route Centers, consisting of 4,000 pieces of hardware and software, including the host mainframe computers that allow air traffic controllers to manage aircraft flying at high altitude
- The Offshore Flight Data Processing System, used to communicate and display positioning and flight plan information for aircraft over the oceans
- The Terminal Doppler Weather Radar System, used to detect microbursts, gust fronts, wind shifts, and precipitation. This system alerts aircraft of hazardous weather conditions around airports and provides advanced notice of changing weather conditions

So how is the FAA doing in fixing their year-2000 problems? The FAA has received harsh criticism and scrutiny throughout most of 1998 for poor planning and lack of progress with year-2000 issues. It has been noted that, at its early 1998 pace, the FAA wouldn't be fully year-2000 compliant until 2009.[10]

More recently, the FAA appears to be making considerable headway. And some experts believe that any problems people experience with regard to air travel will be with delays and the resulting frustration.[11] In July of 1998, the FAA reported completion of year-2000 fixes to 67% of the systems needing work, their internal goal being 60%.[12] FAA Administrator Jane Garvey is so confident that the FAA will achieve year-2000 compliance that she has vowed to fly on a commercial airline to a rather unusual destination—into the next century. She plans to be flying at midnight, December 31, 1999 into January 1, 2000 across all time zones in the United States.[13]

But not all the experts share Ms. Garvey's confidence. There are reports that several federal agencies, including the FAA, has exaggerated their degree of progress. Specifically, the FAA has been criticized for describing as repaired some systems where parts have not yet been received or installed.[14]

Too Much Year-2000 Baggage

A reservation is the starting point in everyone's travel plans. The airlines use enormous computer systems to manage the millions of reservations made each year. Many of these systems are at risk for year-2000 problems—with a twist. Reservation systems are forward looking, making reservations up to a year in advance. So, this is one area where you could have difficulties well before the year 2000. Once we rollover into 1999, non-compliant systems can potentially start to malfunction. You wouldn't want to make a reservation well in advance only to find that the computer system lost your information or had booked you for a 100-year-old, non-existent flight.

If you are dealing with a travel agency, the agency's computer systems must also be compliant. If not, you may need to shop around for an agency that has done their year-2000 homework.

Similarly, airline computer systems are extremely interconnected. They have to be in order to coordinate seating, baggage, and connecting flight information. Because of this interdependency, year-2000 problems introduced by one airline could domino and cause problems for others.[15]

Subways, Buses, and Ferries

Millions of commuters use trains, subways, buses, and ferries as their primary means of getting to and from work as well as for shopping and travel. Amtrak alone carried more than 20 million intercity passengers in 1995[16] and logged 5.1 million miles in 1997.[17] In some areas, public means of transportation are the only ones available. For example, people living on some of the San Juan Islands of Washington rely on the ferry as the only means of transportation to the mainland. If the ferry doesn't run, everyone stays home.

For others, public transportation may be the most economical or convenient choice. Many in New York City, for example, use buses and subways for the simple reason that the cost and hassle of parking a car is prohibitive, not to mention driving adds to the traffic congestion of a big city.

All forms of mass transit, trains, buses, subways and ferries, use computer systems for scheduling, routing and tracking. Some, such as Amtrak, have large reservation systems, and most all use computers to track maintenance and inventory. Just like the airline industry, these systems must be year-2000 compliant for service to continue smoothly.

Since so many people rely on mass transit, why has there been so little discussion of year-2000 concerns? The most likely answer is that mass transit year-2000 problems just haven't captured the attention of the public. The bus that doesn't arrive on schedule pales in comparison to the potential disaster if air traffic control systems don't work. Yet train and subway systems rely on sophisticated computer systems to prevent them from colliding with each other.

Perhaps the lack of year-2000 press for mass transit is a reflection of demographics—often it is the young, elderly, and less affluent who ride the buses and subways. Traditionally, these groups don't have the voice of other segments of the population.

Whatever the reason, there are important year-2000 considerations with mass transit. One expert was quoted as saying that he expected each rail company to have at least one mission-critical failure in ticketing or scheduling.[18] While not catastrophic, the inconvenience, frustration, and confusion created could be significant.

Automobiles

In our society, automobiles are the basic means of transportation. In 1995, American families took nearly 505 million trips of 100 miles or more and logged almost 452 billion miles by car, pickup truck, van, rental car, recreational vehicle, motor home, motorcycle, and moped.[19]

Increasingly, computerized technologies have been making their way not only into automobile manufacturing, but into automobiles themselves, as well. In addition, computerized technologies are used to monitor and manage the millions of vehicles on the road. Can you imagine the traffic jam in any sizable city if the traffic lights were out or operating erratically?

Automobiles: Computer technologies are used to help cars run more efficiently and effectively. Embedded chips are used in electronic fuel injection and ignition systems and help monitor engine functions such as fuel consumption, emissions, engine temperature, and hundreds of other processes. It makes sense to question their year-2000 compliance.

Will cars would stop running at the stroke of midnight or fail to start the morning of January 1, 2000? The answer is no, according to automobile manufacturers. Major American automobile manufacturers Ford, GM, and Chrysler have given their cars a green light for the 21st century.[20]

The answer is no, unless you live in Australia. According to a story that broke in August, 1998, tests of many cars found only one, the Ford Falcon, to have a year-2000 error.[21] However, the problem reportedly will not cause the car to cease to operate or jeopardize car safety and reliability in any way. Rather, the automobile will experience a date-related nuisance problem with its computerized dash display.

Traffic Management: The millions of cars in daily use have led to the need for sophisticated and technologically advanced systems to monitor and manage traffic. Today, computer-driven intelligent traffic-light management systems help speed the flow of traffic in many cities. By minimizing stop-and-go driving, these systems help reduce emissions and lessen the degree of wear and tear on your car. And, hopefully, they make driving in heavy traffic a less frustrating experience.

Many of these traffic-light computers and other systems have year-2000 concerns. Experts have noted that,

> . . .highway safety could be severely compromised because of potential Year 2000 problems in operational transportation systems. For example, date-dependent signal timing patterns could be incorrectly implemented at highway intersections if traffic signal systems run by state and local governments do not process four-digit years correctly.[22]

Some cities are already discovering just this problem. In testing its traffic control computer for year-2000 compliance, the city of Orlando, Florida, found that, after December 31, 1999, programs developed for rush-hour, holiday, and weekday traffic would no longer work.[23] The potential for chaos is obvious.

Foreign Travel

A projected 55.9 million Americans will be travelling abroad in 1999.[24] This is a substantial figure, making it likely that a fair number of Americans will be experiencing year-2000 problems outside the United States. Unfortunately, there appears to be a greater risk for considerable year-2000 problems in other countries for at least two reasons. First, the awareness level of the year-2000 problem is not as high as in the United States. Second, other countries don't have the resources, both in terms of personnel and finances, to apply to year-2000 problems.

What kinds of problems can the traveler expect to encounter outside the United States? The same problems as within the United States. Year-2000 problems are likely to be similar across nations and around the world. The *probability* of having year-2000 problems, however, is the crucial issue. Some countries are more likely to experience, for example, reservation, scheduling, ticketing, customs and immigration problems as well as power outages and/or spikes, healthcare concerns, and downed telecommunications. Safety is a key issue.

Safety: While experts tend to believe that year-2000 travel problems in the United States are more likely to be issues of inconvenience, there is increased concern that the lack of year-2000 preparedness in other countries could manifest as safety issues.

Some airlines are already responding to this concern. Dutch Airline KLM has decided to cancel flights the first week in 2000 if airports can't prove they have fixed their year-2000 problems.[25] For these reasons, the International Air Transport Association (IATA) has donated $20 million to help financially strapped nations fix year-2000 problems plaguing their air-traffic control centers.[26] It is questionable if everyone will be prepared, however.

The United States, Canada, and Britain are commonly reported to be better prepared to address year-2000 problems than are many other countries. These three have established programs, and the level of awareness is relatively high. However, travelers to other areas, such as Southeast Asia, South America, and Africa, need to be aware that progress on year-2000 concerns may lag far behind.

In addition, anyone traveling to a foreign country during this time should also consider the potential difficulties if phone service, power, and healthcare are not available. As with other areas of potential year-2000 risk, some countries may trail far behind the United States, Canada, and Britain in both awareness and ability to address these concerns. Travelers should beware.

Insurance: In some countries, if you have airline problems that are the direct result of year-2000 difficulties you may not be able to pursue a claim.[27] In Australia, new regulations have been added providing for a date-recognition exclusion clause, effectively holding the airlines harmless for any year-2000 problems affecting passengers, just as they exclude claims resulting from acts of God, such as tornadoes. While these regulations are set to expire in August 1999, there is skepticism that they will actually be rescinded. As a result, travelers can't rely on the usual safety nets to help cover losses that may occur. It is likely that exclusions of this type will be enacted in other countries, as well. Travelers need to expect and prepare in advance for problems occurring during this period.

Time for Something Uplifting

Elevators are the poster child for the year-2000 movement. Hardly a story is published or speech given about the year-2000 problem that doesn't include the scenario of elevators quietly removing themselves to the basement and stopping operation at midnight, January 1, 2000. The reason usually cited is that, due to the year-2000 problem, elevators will *think* that 100 years have gone by without having been serviced and, as a precaution, the elevators will take themselves out of service.

While a possibility, the truth of the matter is a bit more complex. The majority, if not all, elevators, in and of themselves, do not measure the need for service based on *time*. Rather, elevators measure their need for service by *usage*. On most elevators, this means a non-electronic counter is forwarded with each trip. However, this is not to say that some newer elevators aren't using electronic means of recording the number of trips made—potentially putting elevators at risk. A number of elevator companies have gone on record stating that their products are not at risk for year-2000 problems or are year-2000 compliant.

The real risk to the usability of elevators, however, comes not from the way elevators are manufactured, but from any third-party hardware or software used to modify or modernize elevators. This includes those elevators that have been connected to a management subsystem or a monitoring

Time Out!

What goes up, must come down. Elisha Graves Otis developed the world's first safety elevator in 1852 and installed the first passenger elevator in New York in 1857. After his death, his sons Charles and Norton continued the family tradition, installing Otis hydraulic elevators in office buildings, hotels and department stores across America. In 1903, the new gearless-traction electric elevator revolutionized building construction, issuing in the age of the high-rise structures. After all, you can't build tall buildings if you can't get people to the top. This new elevator was "engineered and proven to outlast the building itself." It's hard to imagine the skylines of some of the world's great cities without buildings like New York's Empire State Building and World Trade Center, Chicago' John Hancock Center, and Toronto's CN Tower—all customers of Mr. Otis' elevator company.

Source: http://www.nao.otis.com/history.html

subsystem, such as a fire or security monitoring subsystem.[28] If these subsystems track service based on time since last service date and are not year-2000 compliant, then it is possible that elevators could take themselves out of service. From high-rise buildings to hospitals this places individuals requiring the use of elevators at risk for experiencing a real downer when the year-2000 arrives.

The Last Word—Should I Stay or Should I Go Now?

As a society we depend on the mobility that has been one of this century's most remarkable achievements. There are serious year-2000 concerns facing all aspects of our transportation network and a tremendous amount of work remains to be done. However, it does appear that, at least in the United States, the problems we experience will be mostly ones of inconvenience.

The picture may be very different in other countries. There is serious concern regarding the safety of travel in some foreign countries. For many, especially the business traveler or the family planning an overseas vacation, serious consideration must be given to the risks involved.

Year-2000 problems may well challenge our ability to go places with the same freedom we've enjoyed in the past. Some factors will be within our control—and some of us may decide not to travel long distances until year-2000 problems are solved. Other factors may be outside our control—and we may find that we won't have access to public transportation. Entering the millennium could be an interesting ride.

Timely Tips—Guidelines for the Millennium

Everybody has unique transportation and travel needs, so the effect of the year-2000 problem will differ for everyone. To gain an understanding of how you could be impacted by year-2000 travel and transportation problems, you need to have an understanding, first, of the ways you use transportation and, second, of what the likelihood is you will be traveling in the year 2000, especially in January when any year-2000 problems are most likely to make their appearance. Use the following to help assess your transportation risks:

- How often do you travel?
- What is your primary means of travel?
- How far in advance do you typically schedule your trips?
- How do you pay for items, with cash, credit or debitcards, or traveler's checks?
- Do you travel primarily within the United States? Or do you also travel abroad? How frequently?
- Are your trips usually of short duration, a few days, or up to several weeks or longer?

Travel Tips

Flying: consider the following when air travel is your primary means of travel.
- Consider moving some trips forward, in advance of the year 2000, to avoid any headaches or complications that could potentially occur.
- Avoid unnecessary travel in January 2000. There is an increased likelihood of year-2000 problems during this period due to embedded chip technologies. January 2000 is likely to be the period when most year-2000 problems are sorted out.
- If you ticket in advance for travel in January 2000, be aware that there may be year-2000 problems. As a precaution, verify your reservation on a regular basis to make certain that year-2000 problems haven't impacted your flight's schedule or your reservation.
- In the event of scheduling and routing problems, build some cushion into your itinerary by arriving the day before important meetings.
- Because of the FAA's late start in addressing their year-2000 problems, you may want to monitor the FAA's progress as the year 2000 nears. In all likelihood, news of the FAA's progress will be reported as the year 2000 draw closer. To confirm reports, you may want to get supporting information from other sources, such as the Government Accounting Office (GAO), which is likely to continue monitoring the FAA's progress through congressional reports. The GAO web site containing recent reports and testimony can be located at <www.gao.gov>
- As people may be trying to get home before the year 2000 arrives—to avoid being stranded, expect greater that usual traffic in late December.

Foreign Travel: Depending on the destination, travel abroad is more risky due to the late start and slow progress of many year-2000 programs in many countries. As a result, it may be wise to avoid scheduling any personal or business trips in January 2000 because of potential scheduling, hardships and safety-related concerns. However, if you absolutely must travel, here are some suggestions:

- Obtain or renew your passport well in advance of the year 2000.
- Take extra money, cash or traveler's checks, in the event you are stranded for a longer period of time than expected. Avoid reliance on credit cards in the event of power outages, telecommunications problems, or other mishaps that could interfere with the authorization of your purchase.
- Take into account that foreign countries may also be at increased risk for experiencing year-2000 related problems with power, water, delivery of goods, availability of healthcare and the like. You may want to take extra precautions to deal with potential issues.
- Prepare a safety kit that includes water purification tablets and other first-aid supplies.
- Take a flashlight and extra batteries.
- Take some easy-to-store, yet high-nutrition foods.
- Prepare your family or others so that, should problems occur, they know you are safe. Inform them that you made advance preparations in the event of water, transportation, or other potential year-2000 related problems.
- If traveling on vacation, be aware that some tours may be cancelled as some tour operators have been unable to get insurance. Insurance companies are becoming cautious of potential year-2000 mishaps. Don't assume your reservation is a guarantee.

Transportation

There are, and will continue to be, times when we *must* have transportation, whether to pick up the children or to get to the office or a doctor appointment. While we may have several transportation means to select from, we tend to rely on just one. When planning for the year 2000, it is important to consider *all* your options.

Backup Transportation: Have backup means of transportation ready or available if year-2000 problems should result in a longer-term complications or unavailability of major means of public transportation. Some ideas include:
- Organize a car pool in advance so you can depend upon fellow workers, neighbors, or friends for transportation
- Try a new form of transportation. If you usually ride the subway, try the bus
- Move closer to your work, or work closer to your home. Bikes and walking are the methods of transportation virtually guaranteed to be free of the year-2000 bug.

General Transportation Considerations: Here are some general transportation considerations, regardless of the means you use to get around.
- Be cautious using transportation the first few days in January 2000 as this is the time when problems with embedded technology would most likely cause difficulties.
- Be cautious using modes of transportation where accidents would more likely cause serious injury, such as with trains or subways. Buses and cars would be less likely to result in serious accident even though there might be traffic management or scheduling and routing problems.
- Fill up you car ahead of the year 2000. Go into the next century with a full tank of gas should there be power, credit- or debit-card verification, or even fuel delivery problems.
- If possible, take time off during this period to avoid worry about needing to get to and from work at all.

Elevators

While not typically considered as being a mode of transportation, elevators certainly are a device transporting us to a location. For many, elevators are the primary means for getting to the floor of an office or getting home in a high-rise apartment building. Elevators are frequently used in hospitals and airports as well. If elevator usage should be factored into your year-2000 planning, consider the following:
- At apartment high rises, talk to the building manager to determine if year-2000 concerns have been investigated (as well as security, sprinkler, and emergency back up systems). If you are not satisfied with the response

you get, your options may be somewhat limited. However, moving to another building or at least to a lower floor may be a consideration.

- If climbing multiple flights of stairs is a daunting task for you now, think what it would be if you were carrying groceries and other supplies. Make sure you are well prepared before potential elevator problems force you into this situation.

- If your company is located in a high-rise office buildings, its year-2000 assessment plan should include a check of elevator systems. At a minimum, somebody in your office should be in charge of verifying that the building owner or management group has evaluated and addressed general building issues, including year-2000 elevator concerns.

- If all else fails, see your doctor and start an exercise program!

---

[1] Millennium-Asian airlines take off to fight bug. September 4, 1998. *Reuters Business News.* Available from <http://guide-p.infoseek.com/Content?arn=a0184LBY887reulb-19980910&col=NX>

[2] Readiness of Boeing airplanes for Year 2000 operations. Boeing document available at <http://www.boeing.com/commercial/airomagazine/textonly/sy01txt.html>

[3] Kj, Max. 1998. Airbus to cross finishing line. Lexis-Nexis. Available at <http://www.lexis-nexis.com/more/cahners/11373/3753548/17>

[4] Government Accounting Office. 1998. FAA Computer Systems: Limited Progress on Year 2000 Issue Increases Risk Dramatically. Report to Congressional Requesters. Available at http://www.access.gpo.gov/cgi-bin/getdoc.cgi?docid=f:98045.txt.pdf>

[5] Dodaro, Gene L. 1998. Strong Leadership and Effective Public/Private Cooperation Needed to Avoid Major Disruptions. Testimony before the Subcommittee on Government Management, Information and Technology, Committee on Government Reform and Oversight, and the Subcommittee on Technology, Committee on Science, House of Representatives. Available at the GAO web site at <http://access.gpo.gov/cgi-bin/getdoc.cgi?dbname=gao&docid=f:ai98101.txt.pdf>

[6] Same as 4 above.

[7] Thibodeau, Patrick. 1998. IBM wants FAA to retire 3083s. *Computerworld.* Available at http://www.computerworld.com/home/print9497.nsf/all/SL3fly179F6>

[8] Wald, Matthew L. 1998. Warning Issued on Air Traffic Computers. *New York Times*. Available from the *New York Times* web site at <http://www.nyt.com>

[9] Mead, Ken. 1998. Federal Aviation Administration at Risk: Year 2000 Impacts on Air Traffic Control System. Testimony to the Subcommittee on Government Management, Information, and Technology. Available at <http://www.house.gov/reform/gmit/hearings/h980204/km980204.htm>

[10] Horn to Examine Year 2000 Computer Problem at FAA.1998. Press release.

[11] Burnett, Richard. 1998. Bug could gridlock millennial travel. *The Orlando Sentinel*. Available at <http://www.orlandosentinel.com/news/y2k/y2k0829.htm>

[12] McKenna, James T. 1998. Airlines, Agencies Race to Avert Y2K problems. *Aviation Week Online*. <http://www.aviationweek.com/safety/news/nz082498.htm>

[13] *Ibid.*

[14] Wald, Matthew L. 1998. Agencies' Progress on Fixing Year 2000 Problem Is Questioned. *New York Times National Desk Section*.<http://www.nyt.com>

[15] Air travel and Y2K. 1998. *DCI*. Available at <http://year2000.dci.com/articles/1998/09/30air.htm>

[16] National Railroad Passenger Corporation (AMTRAK), available at <http://www.aar.org/comm/statfact.nsf/5406ac733125e6c7852564d000737b60/>

[17] Sames as 14 above.

[18] Same as 11 above.

[19] 1995 American Travel Survey. 1997. U.S. Department of Transportation, Bureau of Transportation Statistics. Available at <http://www.bts.gov/programs/ats/pubs/us/estcus/pdf>

[20] Same as 11 above.

[21] Needham, Kirsty. 1998. Turning feral in 2000. *The Sydney Morning Herald*. Available at <http://www.smh.com.au/icon/980829/cover.html>

[22] Dodaro, Gene L. 1998. Strong Leadership and Effective Public/Private Cooperation Needed to Avoid Major Disruptions. Testimony before the Subcommittee on Government Management, Information and Technology, Committee on Government Reform and Oversight, and the Subcommittee on Technology, Committee on Science, House of Representatives. Available at the GAO web site at <http://access.gpo.gov/cgi-bin/getdoc.cgi?dbname=gao&docid=f:ai98101.txt.pdf>

[23] Same as 11 above.

[24] Tourism Industries International Travel and Forecast for the US, chart 11, ITA Tourism Industries. Available at <http://www.tinet.ita.doc.gov/view/f-109/chart11.html>

[25] Same as 21 above.

[26] Bajak, Frank. 1998. Year 2000 bug could make it vile on Nile, murky in Turkey. *The San Diego Union-Tribune*.

[27] Beer, Stan. 1998. Air travelers may bear bug risk. AFR Net Services. Available at <http://www.afr.com.au/content/980826/inform/inform2.html>

[28] Frequently asked question's - year 2000 compliant products. Otis Elevator Co. Available at <http://www.nao.otis.com/y2k_letter.html>

Chapter 10

Delivery of Goods and the Mail and the Year 2000

In this chapter you will learn:

- How the delivery of goods, mail, and parcels is critical to our daily routine
- How the year-2000 problem could affect rail delivery
- How shipping is at risk for experiencing year-2000 problems
- How satellites are used for everything from navigation of ships to the guidance of missiles

It's the Little Things That Count

We depend on products reaching us from across the country and around the world—products delivered via ship, plane, train, or truck. The sudden lack of availability of even small items, such as paper clips, light bulbs, staples, or that morning cup of coffee, fresh fruit and muffin, could have a profoundly negative effect on the lifestyles to which we have become accustomed. The availability of the little—and big—things are dependent on large delivery systems functioning properly.

The use of computers and automation to assure delivery is extensive. Sophisticated computer systems schedule pickup and delivery, track packages to their destinations, route and schedule trucks and airplanes, and are critical in the navigation of ships.

And more than likely, the delivery of most items require multiple types of transit. Mail, for example, is frequently trucked, flown, and trucked again prior to its delivery to you. Try and imagine a day in which you didn't use something that was delivered to you by truck, train, rail, or plane, or some combination thereof.

- Magazines and newspapers are delivered via air freight and truck.
- Crude oil is delivered by huge cargo ships, eventually to be trucked into individual stations after being processed into gasoline.
- Clothes manufactured overseas are flown in, trucked to a distribution center before being trucked again to the stores in your area.
- The mail you read and the parcels you receive arrive via air, then truck.
- The produce you eat was likely brought in by train, then truck, some of it coming from other countries via cargo ships.
- The coal used to produce the energy to provide air conditioning for your house is delivered by rail.
- The fuel oil used for heating your home is delivered to a local storage facility in tanker trucks or ships, then delivered by truck.
- Medicines prescribed to you by your physician are likely delivered by truck to the pharmacy, which you then pick up using your car.

The list goes on and on. The truth is, we pay little attention to *how* something gets to us—as long as it gets to us. It is not an exaggeration to say that business and government would stop, as would your ability to conduct your daily life, if goods couldn't be transported.

Scoping the Problem—A State of *Un*-readiness

What makes the topic of cargo transit troubling is the current status of the industry. A recent survey by the Special Senate Committee on the year-2000 problem found that three of every five major airlines, railroads, and shipping companies weren't ready. Out of 32 companies targeted for the survey, only 16 responded prior to the hearing on September 10, 1998. Results of the survey included:[1]

- Sixty-two percent of the respondents reported that they had not completed their year-2000 assessment process.
- One-hundred percent of the respondents reported they had not completed contingency plans. Just over half reported that they were *not* working on contingency plans.
- Ninety-four percent reported that their expected year-2000 expenditures would total over $650 million.

- Fifty percent of the respondents reported that they anticipated being involved in litigation due to the year-2000 problem.
- Six out of eight companies answering a question on the percentage of mission-critical systems reported that 70% or more of their systems were critical to their daily operations.

Our dependence on timely and efficient delivery increases just as the global economy seemingly shrinks the distance between countries. The receipt and delivery of products plays an important role in the health of the global economy as well as our daily lives. This chapter explores issues related to the year-2000 problem and delivery systems and how you may be affected.

Mail and Parcels

If you aren't yet persuaded of the importance of delivery and transportation in our lives, these numbers should help convince you. United Parcel Service (UPS) currently employs over 300,000 people in the United States, delivers over 12 million parcels and documents *daily*, and had revenue of $22.4 billion in 1996.[2] Similarly, the United States Postal Service (USPS) currently processes over 600 million pieces of mail *each day*, about 182.7 billion pieces of mail *per year*. If the USPS were a private company, its $56.4 billion in operating revenue would qualify it as the ninth largest business in the United States.[3] Make no mistake, moving letters and packages is big, BIG business.

The high-tech sophistication of these operations is equally impressive. In delivering about 80% of the nation's packages, UPS requires 4,000 people to run a massive computer network that also tracks those 12 million packages

---

The first airmail delivery, February 18, 1911, was made in India, from Allahabad to Naini, a distance of about five miles. A Frenchman named Henri Piquet, flying a Humber biplane, made the flight as a feature attraction of the United Provinces Exhibition. Seven years later, a $100,000 appropriation gave the United States Post Office the means to try experimental air service between New York and Washington. Specially-built aircraft made it possible to extend the service to Chicago in 1919. Airmail services often preceded regular transport of passengers over a given route.

Time Out!

Source: The Encyclopedia of Aviation, Charles Scribner's Sons, New York, 1977, p.8.

---

delivered each day.[4] Likewise, the USPS uses more than 11,500 optical readers and bar code sorters to help in the automation of mail processing.[5] And some of these delivery companies own, operate, and schedule their own fleets of airplanes which more than likely use modern, computerized means of navigation. UPS has a ground fleet of 147,000 vehicles and an air fleet of 197 aircraft, and charters still over 300 more.[6] Likewise, FedEx has more than 600 aircraft in its worldwide air fleet.[7]

Given the size of these operations, it should come as no surprise to learn that there is a lot of computer code, including embedded systems, that needs to be evaluated for year-2000 problems. The potential for great confusion and chaos exists if these systems are not fixed in time.

Lest You Forget ...

You only need to recall the chaos of the United Parcel Service (UPS) strike in late 1997 to recognize the importance of delivery companies. It wasn't that long ago that front-page headlines detailed stories of fresh crab being late for parties and fresh fish not being delivered to destinations on time.

Due to the overload during the strike, many other delivery companies restricted services to existing accounts in order not to compromise their service. This left many other customers with few options. Despite these restrictions, these other companies could not guarantee on-time delivery. Many businesses found themselves stocking up on critical inventories whereas others attempted to find other methods of delivery, even having company employees transport packages. When the UPS strike took place the impact was immediate. There is no reason to believe the impact wouldn't be just as great or as sudden should there be year-2000 problems. Without knowing it, with this recent strike we may have experienced a trial run for what could happen if year-2000 problems impact delivery systems.

Delivery problems resulting from year-2000 non-compliance issues could be exacerbated by the widespread use of just-in-time methods of managing inventory in stores selling products or by manufacturers producing products. Just in time means exactly what it says—that merchandise, components, products, and so on are received just in time for their use in other products or for their sale in stores. This reduces the amount of inventory a company must hold, in turn reducing the amount of capital tied up. In other words, why have a thousand *widgets* on hand when you only need one right now?

Rail Transportation

Railroads transport an enormous amount of goods across the United States. Some quick facts may help to orient you to the size of this means of transport. In the United States there are:[8]

- Over 230,000 miles of railroad track
- About 1.2 million freight cars
- About 20,000 locomotives
- Approximately 89,000 track miles of signal and train control systems

The railroad transports a diverse mix of cargo, including chemicals, foods, forest products, grains, cars/trucks and parts, and metals and minerals. Rail companies connect seaports with the rest of the nation and provide connections to important trading partners, Canada and Mexico.

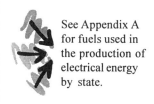

See Appendix A for fuels used in the production of electrical energy by state.

Rail is the major means of transporting coal, a critically important fuel source for the production of energy for the United States. Altogether, coal serves as the basis for 57% of electrical energy production in the United States and as high as 70% in some regions of the country.[9] This underscores

Time Out!

All aboard—and bring your gun! In 1876 the Denver & Rio Grande and the Atchison, Topeka and Santa Fe railroad companies were in hot competition for routes into Colorado and New Mexico. With both companies trying to lay track up the steep canyons to the silver mines in Leadville, Colorado, tempers flared. The Santa Fe hired the famous Bat Masterson along with other lesser gunslingers. The Rio Grande settled for local talent and the state militia. Both sides harassed the other, burning bridges, moving survey stakes, creating avalanches and sniping at work crews. Stockholders of the Rio Grande negotiated a truce and leased the Rio Grande road and equipment to Santa Fe. But an angry J. Palmer, Rio Grande's founder, ordered his men to take back the trains. When the dust cleared, two were dead, and the Rio Grande gang controlled the route to Leadville. Mr. Palmer remarked to his wife, "Amidst all the hot competition of this American business life there is a great temptation to be a little unscrupulous."

Source: Keith Wheeler. The Railroaders. Time-Life Books, New York. 1973, pp. 111.

the importance of rail and the need for systems to operate effectively during the transition to the year 2000.

Given the vast size of the rail system, you might correctly assume that computerized technologies play a large role in keeping it all together. In fact, some rail companies have among the most sophisticated computer and communications networks anywhere. These systems perform many tasks, including the assignment of rail cars and crews, the tracking of shipments, routing, and billing.

Even without a year-2000 type problem, things can get snarled up. Over the past year, the largest railroad in the U.S., Union Pacific, has struggled with a series of problems that resulted in gridlock and confusion. Reports appeared in papers of undelivered products, grain going bad,[10] lost shipments and a total economic loss to the country estimated at over $1 billion.[11] These disruptions in service can play havoc with the needs of suppliers and customers, and can even result in higher prices for products. One report noted that natural gas prices increased 50% in some areas as a result of this gridlock.[12]

While not the result of year-2000 problems, the difficulties experienced by Union Pacific and those depending on timely shipments is an indicator of just how important the rail system is in the United States. Union Pacific has announced their intention to have many of their systems compliant by the end of 1998.[13] And they have a big task. Union Pacific reportedly found that 82.5% of the 12 million lines of executable code would be affected by date-related fields.[14] Let's hope year-2000 programs remain on track for *all* the railroads.

Highways and Byways

Challenges facing over-the-road transportation are no less formidable. Large trucking companies utilize computerized systems to schedule and track shipments and control routing. On the road, intelligent traffic management systems, computerized means of helping direct traffic efficiently, are used in most cities and have their own year-2000 complications. Malfunctions in these systems can create gridlock, stopping even the biggest 18-wheeler. Not only can year-2000 problems in these systems create delivery problems, but they can also present safety concerns. Testimony before the Subcommittee on Technology, Committee on Science, has noted such a possibility, reporting that, "highway safety could be severely compromised because of potential Year 2000 problems in operational transportation systems."[15]

The Shipping Lanes

There was a time when imported goods were rare, when most of the goods needed for daily living were made in the United States. Today, imported goods are standard fare; in fact, it is difficult to tell whether something is imported or not. Domestic cars, for example, contain parts and major components made and assembled from all over the world. Likewise, foreign autos are frequently manufactured in the United States from a mix of overseas and domestic parts. Determining if something is domestic or imported is now based on the percentage of parts from countries and the location of final assembly. This is certainly a measure of just how small and interdependent the world has become.

Delivering the many, myriad products across the seas, shipping is at least partly responsible for the shrinking of our world. Products and merchandise are extremely varied and include everything from crude oil to bananas. Like everywhere else, computer technology in the maritime industry has become ever present, used in any number of capacities from the designing of ships to their navigation across the seas.

There are reports that the maritime transportation industry is behind in fixing their year-2000 problems. Fixing year-2000 problems is important in the maritime industry as ships are increasingly using computerized technology to provide everything from navigation and propulsion to safety controls and refrigeration. With 80,000 ships sailing the world's seas, the risk of collision or other mishap due to failure of computerized technology is increased.[16] This means the potential loss of products and goods being shipped also is increased.

The Problem, Dear Brutus, Lies Not in Our Stars . . .

Ships require accurate navigational systems to deliver their cargo in a timely manner to the right destination. Interestingly, ships today, as in the past, are guided by looking to the heavens. Today, however, the modern maritime industry relies on satellites in the Global Positioning System (GPS) rather than the stars themselves.

The GPS used by so many commercial entities, including modern day shipping, was originally developed by the United States Department of Defense and consists of 24 satellites, three of which are operational spares.[17] The satellites are placed in orbit so that no less than four will be in view anywhere on the face of the earth at any time.[18]

Time Out!

Saddle Up Your Camel. Trade and travel across the vast, barren reaches of the Sahara desert took special skills. Guided by the stars or familiar rocks, pilots led caravans from oasis to oasis and on to their destination. A cargo of gold or salt as well as other goods might be carried on the backs of up to 12,000 camels. And the trip took as long as six months. The wealth from this trade built the west African kingdoms of Ghana, Mali and Songhai.

Source: http://www.n-link.com/-angus/goldtrad.htm

The GPS provides two types of service. The GPS service most used by commercial entities, the Standard Positioning Service (SPS), is reported to provide accuracy within 100 meters horizontally and 156 meters vertically with a time transfer accuracy to within 340 nanoseconds.[19] The GPS service reserved for military use and those authorized by the United States, the Precise Positioning Service (PPS), is reputed to provide exactness to within 22 meters horizontally and 27.7 meters vertically with an improved time transfer accuracy to within 200 nanoseconds.[20] The military makes much use of the GPS, so much so that Tomahawk cruise missiles, called *smart bombs*, use GPS information for precision targeting.[21]

In addition to the usual year-2000 concerns, there is actually a second date-related concern with this technology, the End-of-Week (EOW) rollover problem. The EOW rollover problem deals with the way time is measured. The GPS keeps track of time by counting weeks. With each week that passes, the GPS counter adds one. The number goes as high as 1024, then starts over. The GPS began its count on midnight, January 5th 1980. On midnight, August 21, 1999, a mere 132 days before the arrival of the year 2000, a new cycle will begin as the GPS counter rolls over to one. As a result, many devices not accounting for the rollover may believe that the date is January 5, 1980 instead of August 22, 1999.

It isn't clear how this problem might affect those entities *using* the GPS. However, there has been concern expressed:

Accuracy of navigation may . . .be severely affected. Although it appears that GPS broadcasts do contain sufficient data to ensure that navigation need not be affected by rollover in 1999, it is not proven that the firmware in all receivers will handle the rollovers in stride; some receivers may claim wrong locations in addition to incorrect dates.[22]

There are three segments to the GPS that need to be evaluated to determine compliance with both Y2K and EOW rollover problems:

Space: While the 24 satellites in orbit have been determined to be compliant for the EOW and year-2000 problem, the satellite ground support systems are not year-2000 compliant.[23]

Control: The Control segment of the GPS refers to the five monitoring stations and three ground antennas used to process information to determine the satellite orbits.[24] While originally not compliant for either rollover problem, recent reports indicate that fixes have been made and systems are undergoing validation testing.[25]

User: Some receiver processors used for navigation by the end user (i.e., ships, aircraft, campers) lack year-2000 compliance. Compliance for the year 2000 and for EOW are dependent upon the manufacturers of the equipment. Some receivers are known to lack year-2000 compliance. As such, it is up to the user to insure the compliance of their equipment, for their safety and that of others.

The Last Word—Take Care of the Little Things

The many companies comprising the delivery industry face serious challenges in insuring year-2000 compliance. And, as noted, any company using GPS also has to take into account a separate date-related problem—the EOW rollover problem. Widespread failure due the year-2000 problem in the delivery of goods would have a crippling effect on the health and well being of the economy and would present a serious hardship to millions across the country. We rely heavily on the companies and the various means of delivery they employ for everything from the food we eat to the fuel we use to heat our homes.

So what does this mean to you and me. The good news is we have time to assess the potential impact to ourselves and our families—and make and implement a plan to offset the risks. We may not be able to solve the bigger problems, but we can minimize their effect through the use of just good, common sense.

Timely Tips—Guidelines for the Millennium

Almost everything we use in our day-to-day lives is delivered via truck, train, ship, or plane. Planning and preparation in advance of potential year-2000 problems is important to provide a sense of security and comfort prior to the dawn of the next century.

Impact from delays in the shipping or receiving of supplies will differ, depending on need and circumstance. A modest delay in finding products in stores could be a nuisance for some families. For business, on the other hand, even modest delays can spell serious trouble in conducting business. This may be especially true for those companies whose very livelihood depend on the delivery of goods, such as catalog merchants.

Taking Stock

To prepare for whatever impact year-2000 delivery problems might have on goods you need, track your purchases for all items your buy over a period of time, perhaps a two-week period. The longer the time period, the more likely important items won't be left out. Consider the following as you conduct your assessment:
- Clothing
- Food
- Water
- Fuels, including firewood, propane, and so on
- Medicines
- Cosmetics and personal hygiene items
- Household supplies

Refer to Chapters 2 and 3 for additional information on power, water, and food supplies.

After conducting this assessment, you will have a good idea of what you would need if something happened to delivery systems. If you determine that your situation warrants stocking up on the items you identified, gradually increasing your supplies over time will eliminate last-minute, expensive purchases.

Mail and Parcels

While most families wouldn't be distraught by the loss of mail service and package delivery, businesses would find it very difficult to conduct operations for long. In any event, the following tips will help you to prepare.

- Expect that many people will be sending mail and packages in advance of the year 2000. To avoid problems and delays, plan your holiday mailings well in advance.
- Businesses should learn a lesson from the UPS strike of 1997. Some of the other carriers limited their services to those customers who already had established accounts. If your situation warrants, set up accounts with alternate carriers in advance.
- Keep paper records of the confirmation, tracking, or other numbers used in the delivery of your parcels. As this information is stored electronically, having paper records could help you in the event of a year-2000 mishap.
- If you don't already, insure your packages for loss to protect yourself financially.

---

[1] Senate Y2K Committee Announces Survey Results Measuring Y2K Preparedness of Nations' Largest Transportation Companies, Press Release. United States Senate Special Committee on the Year 2000 Technology Problem. 1998. Available at <http://www.senate.gov/~y2k/news/pr091098.html>. [2]< http://www.ups.com/about/glance.html>

[3] <http://www.usps.com/history/pfact96.htm>

[4] <http://www.ups.com/about/closer-look.html>

[5] <http://www.usps.com/history/pfact96.htm>

[6] <http://www.ups.com/about/closer-look.html>

[7] <http://www.fedex.com/facts_about.html>

[8] Facts from the United States Department of Transportation web site. <http://www.dot.gov/affairs/traind.htm>

[9] See Appendix A for fuels used in the production of electrical energy.

[10] Fairbank, Katie. 1998. Union Pacific sees light at end of gridlocked tunnel. *The San Diego Union-Tribune.*

[11] Cropper, Carol Marie. 1997. As Union Pacific traffic snarls, so do customers. *The New York Times.* Available through the New York Times web site <http://www.nyt.com>

[12] *Ibid.*

[13] Thomas/Bloomerg, Jennifer. 1998. U.S. may ban flights to countries not ready for Y2K, DOT says. *BusinessToday*.com. <http://www.businesstoday.com/techpages/y2kban091098.htm>

[14] Baum, David. 1996. Union Pacific stays on track for 2000. *Datamation*. <http://www.datamation.com/PlugIn/issues/1996/jan1/UnionPacificStays.html>

[15] Dodaro, Gene L. 1998. Strong leadership and effective public/private cooperation needed to avoid major disruptions. Testimony before the Subcommittee on Technology, Committee on Science, House of Representatives.

[16] Howe, Ann. 1998. Y2K poses titanic problems for maritime shipping. *AltaVista MarketSpace*. <http://marketspace.altavista.digital.com/WebPort/English/I-School.asp?Articleid=541&showContent=yes>.

[17] <http://www.laafb.at.mil/SMC/CZ/homepage/space/index.html>

[18] *Ibid.*

[19] <http://tycho.usno.navy.mil/gpsinfo.html>

[20] <*Ibid.*

[21] Slabodkin, Gregory. 1997. What's to be done with GPS? *Government Computing News* (GCN). Available at <http://208.228.76.74/gcn/1997/april14/dod.htm>

[22] <http://www.navcen.uscg.mil/gps/geninfo/y2k/gpsweek.htm>

[23] Christ, Captain Jason. 1998. Year 2000 (Y2K) and GPS end of week (EOW) rollover. PowerPoint presentation available at <http://gps.laafb.af.mil/y2000/y2kbrief.ppt>

[24] <http://tycho.usno.navy.mil/gpsinfo.html>

[25] Same as 23 above.

Chapter 11

Government and the Year 2000

In this chapter you will learn:

- That the U.S. government is the largest buyer of computer technology
- How much the year-2000 problem is going to cost
- What agencies are behind in fixing their year-2000 problems
- That government agencies are highly interdependent and that year-2000 problems affecting one can affect many
- How the IRS is dealing with its year-2000 problem
- That some people have mistakenly been ruled to be in default by the IRS as a result of a bad year-2000 fix

Mortar for a Shaky Foundation

Psychologist Abraham Maslow achieved fame for developing a theory of development called the human hierarchy of needs. As the theory goes, people must first address the lower level, basic needs—food, water, and shelter for example—before pursuing higher level needs, such as developing self esteem or artistic ability. As the lower levels of Maslow's hierarchy of human needs provides for a foundation for people to develop, so government stability provides a foundation for ideals such as liberty and the pursuit of happiness. Without such stability, we would be hard pressed to live life as we have come to know it. Stability is perhaps one of the greatest benefits that government can provide for its citizens. And it is stability that is at risk if the government does not adequately prepare for its year-2000 problems. A government that can't conduct day-to-day business can't provide for its citizens.

Scoping the Problem—Growth Pains

Government was much smaller and simpler for our founding fathers. There were neither computerized systems nor concerns about year-1800 or year-1900 compliance. Government today requires use of a massive complex of interrelated information systems. Both the federal and state governments would be hard pressed to function at all without technology. Yet it is this very technology that may threaten the ability of the government to continue to function properly.

Many have expressed concern that the United States Government will not be adequately prepared when the year 2000 comes:

- "We know that there will be programs that fail and, therefore, a chance that government payments will not be made. The problem, of course, is that we do not know which programs will fail, what problems their failures will create, and how disastrous will be the consequences. Unfortunately, the real problem is that the agencies don't know either."[1]
- "The year 2000 problem represents a threat to systems that are critical to the functioning of the government."[2]
- "The public faces the risk that critical services could be severely disrupted by the Year 2000 computing crisis."[3]
- "At the current pace, it is clear that not all mission critical systems will be fixed in time."[4]

Why such concern? After all, the government faces the same hurdles as any large-sized business reliant on technology, right? The answer is yes, and no. Yes, the government faces the same difficulties as any business dealing with a large network of information systems. No, it is not the same because the size and extent of the problem makes fixing the problem much more difficult. In addition, the government faces some unique challenges. This chapter

Time Out!

Ever wonder just how much the federal government collects in revenue? In 1901 the total receipts were a modest $588 million. Now hang on to your hat—in 1997 the government took in $1.579 trillion!

And how much did the federal government spend? In 1901, there were $525 million in expenditures, leaving a tidy sum of $63 million surplus. In 1997, the outlay was $1.601 billion. And the government went in the red to the tune of $21 billion.

Source: http://www.access.gpo.gov/su_doc/budget/index.html, Budget for Fiscal Year 1999, Historical Tables.

will focus on five complications the government must deal with effectively to achieve year-2000 compliance: magnitude, organizational differences, resources, interdependence, and politics.

Magnitude

The government is dealing with the problem of magnitude in several areas. The United States government is the largest customer of information technology in the country, and possibly the world. It is dependent on computer technology at all levels of government, from military defense to basic public services. We can get an idea of the enormity of the problem if we look at it from a monetary point of view.

Cost estimates to fix year-2000-related problems for mission-critical systems have been steadily increasing and have more than doubled since February 1997. Current estimates from the Office of Management and Budget have come in at $5.4 billion—up from the initial cost estimate of $2.3 billion in February, 1997, the $3.8 billion estimate in August, 1997, and the $4.7 billion estimate in February, 1998. Even the latest estimate of $5.4 billion is expected to rise as we near the end of 1999 when the true costs become more clear. In fact, the House Subcommittee on Government Management, Information, and Technology has estimated the current cost to fix the federal government year-2000 problem at $6.3 billion.[5] The final cost for fixing the year-2000 problem, however, won't be known until well into the year-2000 or beyond as year-2000 expenses will continue well after the current effort to fix the mission-critical systems.

Of course, the federal government is only part of the equation when looking at the size of the problem. State governments are also struggling with year-2000 problems. The current estimate to fix state government problems stands at nearly $5 billion.[6] Combined, the total price tag comes to nearly $10 billion—and it is climbing. Why?

• *Aging systems*: An aging computer system adds complexity to achieving year-2000 compliance. The United States has always been one of the first customers to buy computer technology, in many cases for military purposes. Not only are these systems quite old, the documentation is poor, if it exists at all. In addition, many of these systems may use languages that are not in use today, and the specialists who can decipher them are few. Ideally, the government would simply replace these systems; however, this may not be possible in all circumstances.

• *Ability to Meet Deadlines*: Adding to the magnitude of the problem is the government's poor track record in meeting deadlines. One such example is the IRS's Tax Systems Modernization (TSM) project in which the IRS attempted to update and upgrade many of its computer systems. After a decade of missed deadlines and approximately $4 billion, the project was terminated.[7]

Consequently, the combination of a fixed, immutable deadline with the complexity, size, and age of the government's information systems puts achieving compliance at high risk.

Organizational Differences

Another major problem the government faces in fixing its year-2000 problem deals with organizational differences among its many departments and agencies. The Federal Government is made up of many levels, with many chiefs, directors and managers overseeing their own piece of the governmental pie. Consequently, there are many different approaches to fixing the year-2000 problems.

The Subcommittee on Government Management, Information, and Technology monitors twenty-four federal departments and agencies for their

Time Out!

My Kingdom For A Horse—With Stirrups   Who would have thought that the invention of the stirrup could bring about a change in government. Medieval France was under attack by raiding barbarians and no government forces were able to stop them, until the local Frankish lords developed the ultimate weapon, heavily armored cavalrymen on large horses carrying heavy lances. These knights could exert an enormous force that could easily break through any other military formation of the day. But without the stirrup to push against, the shock of impact would throw the rider to the ground—no stirrups, no knights. Since it took many knights to stop the barbarian raiding, and equipping even one took a lot of money, the surplus of many villages was dedicated to the maintenance of these warriors. Once this force was in place, most villages of Western Europe came under control of these fighting men—the feudal system of government had been born.

Source: William H. McNeill. A World History, Oxford University Press, Oxford, 1979, pp.235-6.

Federal Agency Grades Given by Congress

Federal Department or Agency	Estimated Year Completed	May 15, 1998 Grade
Social Security Administration	1999	A+
General Services Administration	1999	A-
Federal Emergency Management Agency	1999	A-
National Science Foundation	1999	A-
Department of Commerce	1999	B
Small Business Administration	1999	B
NASA	1999	B
Nuclear Regulatory Commission	1999	B
Department of the Treasury	1999	C
Housing and Urban Development	1999	C
Department of Labor	1999	C
Department of Veterans Affairs	2000	C
Office of Personnel Management	2000	C-
Department of the Interior	2001	C-
Department of Agriculture	2000	D
Department of Defense	2002	D
Department of Justice	2000	D
Department of Education	2002	D
Environmental Protection Agency	2006	F
Department of State	2005	F
Department of Health and Human Services	2003	F
Department of Energy	2004	F
Department of Transportation	2004	F
Agency for International Development	2019	F

Source: Subcommittee on Government Management, Information, and Technology, June 2, 1998 report

year-2000 progress. Every quarter, the twenty-four groups receive *grades*, much like the kind given in school. Overall, for every quarter since the monitoring began, it's evident that the federal government as a whole isn't making the grade. As the above list illustrates, tremendous variability exists among the agencies in achieving year-2000 compliance, with some agencies doing much better than others.

Some believe that year-2000 progress in the government is uneven because there is no single, over-arching organization to coordinate and oversee the problem. One government report observed that other countries are doing a better job in this area than the United States: "Other countries have set up mechanisms to solve the Year 2000 problem on a nationwide basis. Several countries, such as the United Kingdom, Canada, and Australia, have appointed central organizations to coordinate and oversee their government's responses to the Year 2000 Crisis."[8] Likewise, regarding U.S. progress, a renowned economist stated that, "no one is setting national priorities and preparing national contingency plans."[9]

Unfortunately, the lack of overall strategy combined with uneven progress raises the risk—there just isn't enough time left to fix the problems.

Resources

A lack of trained personnel is a major obstacle the government faces in achieving year-2000 systems compliance. It is somewhat ironic that it takes old-fashioned people power and smarts to fix the technology problems that we face. Unfortunately, the availability of those with the technical expertise and experience to fix these problems is subject to the forces of supply and demand. Many of these individuals gravitate toward the higher paying jobs in the private sector, leaving government needs unmet.

Government salaries rarely match those found in the private sector. Unfortunately, this could mean trouble for the government's effort to fix its year-2000 non-compliant systems because there could be too few people to assess and fix these problems. One government report commented that a number of agencies are already finding it difficult to hire and keep qualified individuals, leaving a few people to repair, in some circumstances, tens of thousands of application programs and computer systems.

As a result, the government has turned to third parties to assess and fix problems. But this strategy has not proved to be completely effective. For example, the United States Navy contracted with a vendor to fix year-2000 problems. While the Navy was told the system was fixed, testing of the program determined, in fact, it was not.[10] Unfortunately, the lack of trained personnel means that many systems may not be properly tested for compliance. In many circumstances, there are no validation procedures yet devised, and this aspect of making systems year-2000 compliant is among the most time intensive.

Interdependence

Extensive interconnectedness between Federal, State, and outside agencies is another problem facing the government in fixing its year-2000 problems. Few, if any, government agencies operate independently. One of the major concerns deals with the ability of data exchange systems to communicate with each other. Data exchange systems, simply stated, are the systems involved in the electronic transfer of information. This happens through direct computer links, computer linkages via telephone lines and the Internet, and the sharing of data through floppy disks.[11]

The importance of secure and accurate transmission of data cannot be overemphasized. If these systems do not function correctly the result could be serious disruptions in government services.[12] Here is a brief list of some of the areas that could be impacted:

- Collection of data for determination of eligibility for Veterans Administration, Social Security, and Medicare benefits
- Sharing of weather information for air-flight safety or to the U.S. Coast Guard for the planning of search and rescue operations
- Processing of payments through the banking system
- Facilitation of import and export shipments through ports of entry
- Transfer of funds to government contractors
- Inability to compute and/or pay benefits
- Inability for states to receive information from the National Highway Traffic Safety Administration, potentially resulting in licenses being issued to those with revoked or suspended licenses in other states
- Non-availability of information needed by the Nuclear Regulatory Commission from nuclear reactors needed to initiate emergency response actions

According to a report issued by the Government Accounting Office in July 1998, the year-2000 compliance of these important date transmission systems is poor or unknown.

About half of the federal agencies reported during the first quarter of 1998 that they have not yet finished assessing their data exchanges to determine if they will be able to process data with dates beyond 1999. Two of the 39 state-level organizations reported having finished assessing their data exchanges. For the exchanges already identified as not Year 2000 ready, respondents reported that little progress has yet been made in completing key steps such as reaching agreements with partners on date formats, developing and testing bridges and filters, and developing contingency plans for cases in which Year 2000 readiness will not be achieved.[13]

Each agency must try to protect the billions of bits of data, data about you and me, in its computers from the effects of non-compliant systems. For example, if the Social Security Administration solved their internal year-2000 problem, but another department with whom it shared data had not, the Administration data could be corrupted as well. This would mean the Administration was, for practical purposes, not much better off than before it spent millions of dollars in preparation for the year 2000. Corrupted data can sit in databases for years before being recognized as inaccurate. And worse yet, corrupted data could spread like a virus, corrupting data in other government databases until there are tremendous, widespread inaccuracies. In turn, this would impact all those individuals who need services, potentially delaying funds or assistance.

The Game of Politics

The fifth general year-2000 issue facing the government is politics. Or, more accurately stated, the game of politics. Because the scope of the year-2000 problem is so great, some government officials may be tempted to turn it into a political issue. Already, newspaper articles are detailing how political parties are planning to use the year-2000 problem to their political advantage. Unfortunately, this means there could be less incentive to repair the government's serious year-2000 problems. This is a dangerous game, and one not in the best interest of the country.

The Internal Revenue Service (IRS)

While this chapter has been devoted to general problems affecting all government agencies, there is a need to specifically address the year-2000 status of the IRS. The IRS is the agency responsible for collecting taxes from individuals and business, which in turn provides funding for government programs and services. In 1996, the IRS collected over a trillion dollars.[14]

In fixing its year-2000 problems, the IRS has one of the most difficult jobs facing any government agency. The task includes analyzing 62 million lines of computer code in 88,000 programs on 80 mainframe computers.[15] In addition, the IRS must assess at least 130,000 personal computers and 60,000 pieces of telecommunications equipment.[16] While the initial cost estimate in February 1997 was $129 million, the estimate soon ballooned to nearly a $1 billion—$850 million through 1999 with additional costs expected in the year 2000.[17] Further complicating the IRS' difficulties is the need to enact approximately 800 tax changes passed by Congress.[18]

Risks to the government are high if the IRS fails to fix its year-2000 problems in time. In jeopardy are the core computer systems that process 200 million tax returns yearly.[19] Perhaps your first response to this information was to feel that the IRS is getting its just desserts, but the effects go far beyond the possibility that our personal tax returns might not be processed. Failure of these systems also jeopardizes the collection of revenue and the ability of government to pay for programs and services. Unfortunately, these are also the computer systems that cut refund checks for thousands of Americans.

The IRS has already stated that some of their computer systems will not be ready by the year 2000. If this weren't bad enough, a few of the IRS fixes are causing some taxpayers to have headaches. About 1000 people, current in their tax installment agreements, were declared in default as the result of a bad year-2000 repair.[20] For these individuals as well as the IRS, the year-2000 problem is proving to be very taxing indeed.

The Last Word—The Year-2000 Problem is No Yankee Doodle Dandy

The difficulties facing the government in fixing its year-2000 problems are serious. Progress has been mixed with some departments likely to complete fixes only to their mission-critical systems, while, at the current pace, others will not reach even this minimum level of year-2000 preparedness.

At this point, it looks as though many portions of the government will not be ready when the year 2000 arrives. As this fact becomes more apparent, we will probably see an increase in the development of contingency plans to try and maintain what has been referred to as *minimally acceptable levels*

Turn of the Century Trivia:In 1800, John Adams led the U.S. into the new century—Adams held office from 1797 to 1801. In 1800, the U.S. was comprised of 16 states. In 1900, President William McKinley led the U.S. into the new century—he held office from 1897 to 1901. At that time, the U.S. was comprised of 44 states. The U.S. will enter the next century with 50 states. It was during Dwight D. Eisenhauer's office that the last two states—Hawaii and Alaska, were added.

Time Out!

Source: New Encyclopedia Brittanica, Vol 12, p. 153. Encyclopedia Britannica, Chicago. 1973 and New Book of Knowledge, Grolier Inc., 1983. Danbury, CT, Vol. 19, pp 90-93.

of service. The result of this minimization of service, at a practical level, is likely to mean reduction in services to people.

Should this result in a return to hand processing of forms, billing, authorizations and the like, this would lead to a slowdown of massive proportions. On a practical level, it would mean a reduction of services we have come to take for granted.

What does that mean for you and me? Good, old-fashioned ingenuity. Time to roll up our sleeves and take preventative measures.

Timely Tips—Guidelines for the Millennium

Almost everybody interacts with the government at some time in varying degrees. The fact is, most people aren't aware of just how much we depend on the government, both state and federal, for benefits, funds, or other services. Following are just a few of the services that millions of citizens depend on:

- Social Security benefits
- Medicare and Medicaid benefits
- Welfare, food stamps, and unemployment benefits
- Student loans and grants for education
- Housing assistance
- Passports for travel outside the United States

Aside from services, we also depend on the government *to process* documents correctly. Few would be happy to discover errors in their Personal Earnings and Benefits Estimate Statements (PEBES), information collected by the Social Security Administration. We also expect the IRS to process our tax statements correctly and distribute refund checks.

The fact is, if you receive benefits, services, funds, or have any interaction with government agencies, you might want to take a few steps to prevent complications.

Archive Important Documents

When preparing for potential year-2000 problems with the government, make hard copies of important documents to verify status, funds, benefit eligibility, and the like. Do not depend on government agencies to keep track of all the pertinent facts about you. The following list will provide guidance for the types of records you may want to archive.

- Social Security cards
- Tax returns
- Student loan records
- Personal Earnings and Benefit Estimate Statements (PEBES)
- Veteran's Administration benefit information
- Medicare and Medicaid Benefit information
- Unemployment information
- Passports

To be easily accessible, records should be well organized and kept in a safe place. Depending on how risk averse you are, you may want to make a second copy of these documents to be stored in a different location. Much of this information can be gathered by contacting each specific agency, often via web sites. In the case of the PEBES, for example, you would go to the Social Security Administration (SSA) web site at <www.ssa.gov> and complete the appropriate form. If you don't have Internet access, you can call the SSA's toll-free number and request a copy of form SSA-7004. Once you have collected this information, you will want to keep it current.

Receiving Benefits

Many people receive benefits from the government. There is some concern that the year-2000 problem could cause an interruption in benefit payments. If you rely on these benefits, it's important to collect pertinent records and information to show your eligibility status and history. If possible, you may want to save what money you can as a reserve in case benefit payments are delayed. Advance planning and stored reserves of needed supplies and foodstuffs can also help alleviate potential problems.

For tips on storing food, see Chapter 3, *Food and the Year 2000*.

---

[1] Horn Grades Federal Government on the Year 2000 Problem. 1997. Press release from the Subcommittee on Government Management, Information, and Technology. Available at <http://www.house.gov/reform/gmit/press/p970915.htm>

[2] Government Accounting Office. 1998. Continuing Risks of Disruption to Social Security, Medicare, and Treasury Programs. Testimony before the Subcommittee on Oversight, Committee on Ways and Means, House of Representatives. Available at <http://www.www.access.gpo.gov/cgi-bin/getdoc.cgi?dbname=gao&docid=f:ai98161t.txt.pdf>

[3] Same as 1 above.

[4] Dodaro, Gene L. 1998. Strong Leadership and Effective Public/Private Cooperation Needed to Avoid Major Disruptions. Testimony before the Subcommittee on Government Management, Information and Technology, Committee on Government Reform and Oversight, and the Subcommittee on Technology, Committee on Science, House of Representatives. Available at
<http://www.access.gpo.gov/cgi-bin/getdoc.cgi?dbname=gao&docid=f:ai98101.txt.pdf>

[5] Clausing, Jen.1998. U.S. deserves "D" grade on millennium bug, new report says," *New York Times* on the Web <http://www.nytimes.com/library/tech/98/09/cyber/articles/ 10millennium.html>

[6] Action Needed on Electronic Data Exchanges. Report to Congressional Requesters. 1998. Available at http://www.gao.gov/cgi-bin/ordtup.pl?Item0=AIMD-98-124>

[7] Barr, Stephen. 1997. Taking On IRS's Taxing Computer Problems. *The Washington Post*.

[8] Dodaro, Gene L. 1998. *Strong Leadership and Effective Public/Private Cooperation Needed to Avoid Major Disruptions*. Testimony before the Subcommittee on Government Management, Information and Technology, Committee on Government Reform and Oversight, and the Subcommittee on Technology, Committee on Science, House of Representatives. Available at
<http://www.access.gpo.gov/cgi-bin/getdoc.cgi?dbname=gao&docid=f:ai98101.txt.pdf>

[9] Ante, Spender. 1998. Clinton Too Late on Y2K? *Wired News*.

[10] Government Accounting Office. 1998. Defense Computers: Year 2000 Computer Problems Put Navy Operations at Risk. Report to the Secretary of the Navy. Available at <http:// www.access.gpo.gov/cgi-bin/getdoc.cgi?dbname=gao&docid=f:ai98150.txt>

[11] Government Accounting Office. 1998. Action Needed on Electronic Data Exchanges. Report to Congressional Requesters. Available at http://www.gao.gov/cgi-bin/ ordtup.pl?Item0=AIMD-98-124>

[12] *Ibid.*

[13] *Ibid.*

[14] General Accounting Office. 1998. IRS Faces Challenges in Measuring Customer Service. Report to the Chairman, Subcommittee on Oversight, Committee on Ways and Means, House of Representatives. Available
<http://www.access.gpo.gov/cgi-bin/getdoc.cgi?dbname=gao&docid=f:gg98059.txt.pdf>

[15] Wells, Rob. 1997. If computer geeks desert, IRS codes will be ciphers. Washingtonpost.com .<http://www.washingtonpost.com/wp-sÉte/1997-12/24/0611-122497-idx.html>

[16] Gleckman, Howard. 1998. Hey, I owe 99 years in back taxes! *Business Week*.

[17] Lewis, Nicole. 1998. *I*RS' tab for year 2000 fix to total nearly $1 billion. *Federal Computer Week*. <http://www.fcw.com/ref/hottopics/y2k/web-irs-4-15-1998.html>

[18] Herman, Tom. 1998. Tax Report: the IRS struggles to avoid meltdown from the dreaded year-2000 bug. *The Wall Street Journal Interactive Edition*. <http://interactive.wsj.com/ articles/SB907102750736505000.htm>

[19] Wells, Rob. 1997. IRS says its computer overhaul for year 2000 to cost $129 million. *New York Times on the Web*. Available at cost from the archives at *The New York Times*, <http:/ /www.nyt.com>

[20] Wells, Rob. 1998. IRS fix on 2000 bug sends taxpayers into 'default'. *Seattle Post-Intelligencer*.

Part Two

Chapter 12

Maggie and the Year 2000

About Maggie:

- Thirty-seven years old
- Single home owner who lives in California
- Small business owner
- Elderly parents live in New England

Maggie—My Thoughts

I've always been somewhat of a risk taker—I would never have taken on the challenges of owning my own importing business otherwise. I like being independent and making my own decisions. My approach to the year-2000 problem is similar to the way I approach any business obstacle—gather information, make a plan, and take action.

After reading about the year-2000 problem, I decided that preparation was key to managing any potential problems. Among the first things I did was to determine the primary source of electrical energy production for my home and business in California. Electricity in California seems to be pretty evenly divided between hydroelectric (38%), nuclear (29%), and gas (26%). While I personally am not too worried about the loss of power from hydroelectric and gas sources, I am concerned about the unknown risk involved in making sure nuclear power plants are year-2000 compliant. If we lost nuclear power as a source of electricity production because of safety concerns, I don't know where we would make up that 30%. Because I live in southern California, I'm not concerned about extremely cold winter temperatures, but I do plan to look at alternate light and cooking sources, maybe a Coleman lantern and camp stove.

I also decided to stock up on some food supplies. I'm so busy running my business that I rarely have time to cook. I eat a lot of frozen dinners and take out from the Chinese restaurant up the street. In talking about this issue with some of my friends and employees, we decided to form a group to investigate nutritional needs, what types of food store well, and the cost of bulk and ready-to-eat foods. We generally agreed that it would be good to have about a six-months supply on hand. Since I have a large garage, I offered to store some food for members of the group that don't have enough space in their own homes. And since we'll be stocking many of the same foods, we decided to buy in bulk and case lots to save money. We'll be making some of the buying decisions at our next monthly meeting.

I do have some concerns about water and the year-2000 problem. Southern California generally has a dry climate, and in Los Angeles where I live, there are few sources of water other than the public utility system. I've always been particular about how water tastes, so I get my drinking and cooking water from a supplier that delivers water in five-gallon containers. I have decided to store a month's worth of water, or around 30 gallons. My water delivery person told me to expect the water to have a shelf life of about two years, *if* I keep the bottles out of the sun and in a cool place. I figure I should have taken this precaution some time ago since I live in an earthquake-prone area. I'll also be storing several five-gallon containers at work for our needs there. In September 1999, I plan to reassess whether I want to store even more water to insure supplies for a longer period of time.

One of my big concerns had to do with my home. I just bought a lovely three-bedroom Craftsman-style bungalow and am carrying a hefty mortgage. While I would love for the bank to have a computer glitch when the year 2000 arrives and somehow show that I've paid off my loan, I'm not holding my breath. Just in case it goes the other way and the bank somehow thinks I haven't made a payment for a hundred years, I'm keeping a well-organized file on my account and all the mortgage payments that I've made.

My Business

Living in Southern California where winters are mild, I'm not very worried about the inability to heat my office, should worse come to worse and power sharing were instituted. I am concerned, however, about running my business if we have power outages. We depend on our computers for many things, from taking catalog orders over our web page to keeping track of inventory. Thankfully, half of my computers are year-2000 compliant Macintosh systems. Of the other four, all passed the compliance tests except for one. I've decided to take the non-compliant computer out of service altogether. I'd rather not spend the money replacing it unless I have to, so we'll try to make do with what we have. I'm also planning a thorough assessment of all my computer applications and databases.

I'm also concerned about spikes in the power supply. I have a lot of money invested in equipment. It seems to me that one of the easiest ways to protect this investment is to purchase surge-protection devices that have battery backups which will allow us a few minutes to shut down our equipment and programs safely.

My web page is an important part of my business. If people can't access it, I don't make sales. I contacted the Internet service provider that maintains my web presence to find out what contingency plans are in place in case power goes down. They had none. So, I'm in the process of switching to an ISP that has a mirror site in another part of the country. Although this new ISP doesn't have a backup generator, having some redundancy makes me feel a little better in the event we experience regional power problems. I plan to revisit this issue later just to see if a better solution comes available.

Telecommunications is another area of concern to me, especially in my kind of business. I rely heavily on the Internet for receiving orders, but I also have customers who subscribe to my quarterly catalog and submit orders by phone and fax. I'm also in frequent communication with suppliers overseas, especially in South America and Southeast Asia. And I have several employees who travel throughout these regions looking for products we can sell. They stay in close touch with me about purchasing new inventory.

As it's hard for me to know exactly what products will be *hot* in the first half of 2000, I want to postpone making some buying decisions for as long as possible, yet allow sufficient time to receive the products well before the end of 1999. While my suppliers are decidedly low tech, I am concerned that year-2000 problems with transportation to and from these overseas regions may make it difficult for my suppliers to fill and ship orders. And I have decided that, as things stand now, it is not worth the risk sending my buyers overseas during the December 1999 - January 2000 period.

As part of my contingency planning, I decided to increase the level of cash available for my business—a reserve to get me through a dry spell in case I can't sell products or don't have products to sell. With this in mind, I plan to have a very lean and efficient operation.

Getting my products to customers is also a concern. I learned the hard way during the UPS strike that I need to have a backup plan. My employees and I spent a lot of time taking packages to the Postal Service. It's more efficient to have packages picked up at the office, so I've established an account with two additional carriers so that I don't find myself in a similar situation at the turn of the century.

My Parents

While I am not concerned about myself and loss of electricity and heat, I am concerned about my parents who live in New England. Living there all their lives, they're pretty hardy folk. But they're getting older, and my father has heart problems.

It concerns me that the largest portion of the Northeast's electricity production comes from nuclear sources. If it would be difficult to make up for the 30% loss of nuclear electric power here in California, imagine what would happen in New England if nuclear power stations go offline.

From my point of view, having my parents spend the winter in Los Angeles with me, or with my sister and her family in Miami, would be the best option. However, Mom and Dad don't want to leave their home for so long a stay. We'll continue to discuss options for a while longer, but we've all agreed that we need to come to some decision no later than summer of 1999. In the meantime, my sister and I are researching year-2000-ready healthcare providers, such as pharmacies, medical clinics and nursing facilities, near our parents' home, just in case Dad's heart condition worsens and it's not possible for him to travel. My sister and I are also considering hiring someone to help get Mom and Dad prepared for winter, supplying extra firewood and the like. It would probably be worthwhile to arrange for a friend or someone else to check in on them regularly, too, just to see how they are doing. If for some reason we couldn't call each other, it would give me some peace of mind knowing someone was seeing to their needs.

The Final Word

Overall, I feel pretty good about the decisions I've made thus far regarding the year-2000 problem. I know that as we approach the turn of the century more information will be available about what to expect. So I intend to monitor the areas that concern me, my family, and my business and take action as things become clearer. In any case, I intend to be as ready for the year 2000, and whatever it brings, as I can possibly be.

Chapter 13

Dale and Patty and the Year 2000

About Dale and Patty:

- Married for nearly 35 years
- Nearing retirement
- Live in the northwest part of the United States
- Patty experiencing health problems

Dale—My Thoughts

Patty and I both remember our parent's stories about the great depression and the measures their families had to take just to survive. I guess you could say those stories made an indelible impression on us because we've always been cautious with our money. It seems that we've been saving for retirement all our lives. Now that we are close to that point, we don't want to let anything take away from us what we've worked so hard to get.

During my career, I worked for a couple of the big high-tech companies headquartered here in the northwest, so I'm certainly familiar with computers and software—and resulting problems when the things don't work right. These experiences coupled with my family history have probably made me a bit risk averse—especially when it comes to money.

After talking with our investment advisor about this year-2000 issue, Patty and I decided to reallocate most of our retirement funds into low-risk investments. If we can protect our core savings, we can manage just fine. We've also decided to keep some money where we could have access to it quickly. My parents told me stories about keeping a few dollars hidden throughout the house during *the hard times—even in their car*, because, as my Dad would say, "You just didn't know where and when you might need a little cash." I'm not sure if I want to go that far, though, because of the risk of keeping money about. But Patty and I did decide to buy a fireproof safe and agreed on an amount to keep in it—not necessarily a *whole lot*, but we like the idea of being able to put our hands on cash if we need to. We also decided to keep nothing bigger than $20 dollar bills because any bigger and it could get hard for people to give you change back.

Also, because Patty and I believe in self sufficiency regardless of what happens, we decided to have some other forms of currency. On the advice of our investment advisor, we bought some gold and silver coins and have them stored in our safe as well. My kids think that I'm going a bit overboard with this part of the plan, but they just didn't grow up with the concerns that their mother and I did.

When it comes to power supply, we plan to buy a portable generator and keep some extra fuel in the shed. This way we can continue to have some means of heat and refrigeration if we lost power. I personally am not so worried about our power supply here in the northwest but I do wonder if some of our power could be transferred to other parts of the country should something serious happen to other types of power supplies.

Patty—My Thoughts

My mother always kept a full pantry and saved everything, even aluminum foil and rubber bands. I guess I followed in her footsteps, because I have always been pretty frugal. Dale and I have always tried to be somewhat self-sufficient. We've always kept a small organic garden, and I canned fruits and vegetables for the family—partly because we are conservative, but also because we prefer foods that haven't been treated with a lot of chemicals or pesticides. People tell me my blackberry jam is legendary. I learned to make it from my mother. Blackberries—all kinds of fruit—grow wild here in the northwest, so there's always an ample supply. The climate here is good for fruit growing and gardening.

Since we are believers in self sufficiency, Dale and I intend to plant a larger garden this coming summer, and I plan to can more than I usually do. I've already started looking at seed company catalogs, and have even ordered some heirloom seeds. We would like to harvest some of the seeds for planting in following years, and you just can't do that with hybrids. I've developed a plan that will allow us to have enough food for at least a year. We're also encouraging our grown children to become self-sufficient, because you just don't know what can happen sometimes.

In addition to canning some of our own foods, I watch for specials at the local supermarket on products that keep well, such as canned tuna, rice, beans, lentils and flour. When I spot a good deal, I buy a little extra and store it in my year-2000 storage areas, a couple of the closets in the children's old rooms. Dale and I have been discussing whether or not we wanted to buy some non-electric appliances, such as a grinder along with a bulk purchase of corn for making corn meal. But we haven't quite decided how or where we would store all the corn in a way that would prevent insects and pests from getting into it. And because it rains so much here in the Seattle area, especially during the wintertime, we're concerned about keeping the meal good and dry. We're thinking it might do okay in airtight bags within some larger plastic trash containers kept up off the floor in the garage.

I've talked with my doctor about what he's doing to prepare for the year-2000-problem. I've also been putting together an emergency healthcare kit for Dale and me, with such things as:

- copies of both Dale's and my prescriptions
- an extra pair of eyeglasses for each of us in case something happens to our main pair
- a first-aid kit
- extra toothbrushes, toothpaste, and dental floss
- soap, towels, and personal hygiene items

I also wanted to make sure that our important paperwork was in order. I've taken care of the bills and money for the last fifteen years, keeping records of everything from our tax returns to our bank statements. These will go in the safe, along with our investment portfolio records. I've taken care to collect all our important benefits papers, including our Personal Earnings and Benefit Estimate Statements from the Social Security Administration, too. And our birth certificates, marriage license, and social security cards will also go into the safe. Just to be on the safe side, we decided to make a second copy of some of these documents and keep them in a safe-deposit box at the bank.

The Final Word

We grew up during times when you had to depend on yourself and your family to help get you by. In many ways we see the preparation for the year 2000 as no different than what you would do to prepare for any natural disaster. The important thing is to be prepared—it buys peace of mind during tough times.

Chapter 14

John and Teresa and the Year 2000

About John and Teresa:

- Married with two young children
- John's work requires frequent travel
- Concerns about parents' well-being

Teresa—My Thoughts

John and I discussed the year-2000 situation and decided that, even if only minor difficulties occur, it's worth investing in peace of mind, especially since John is away frequently on business trips. Since I bear most of the child-rearing responsibilities, we've decided to let my level of comfort be our year-2000 guideline.

John and I divided the work of preparing for the year-2000 problem. One of my biggest concerns, and the year-2000 responsibility that I wanted to assume, dealt with making sure I could feed our family. I felt we needed to have enough food to last for a six-month period. I did some research at the local library, plus I ordered some government pamphlets on nutrition. I wanted to make sure that I calculated the right kinds of food we needed *and* the right amount. Over the next six months, we will purchase what we need gradually until we have six months of food supplies. I plan to shop at one of the local warehouse-type stores that sells cases of canned goods. There is also a food cooperative in town where I can make bulk purchases of things like rice and beans. We think this method will work well and won't strain our budget too much.

I also want to make sure that we have the ability to cook the food in the event there are electricity outages. We planned for a fireplace in our new house, but I felt it just wouldn't be very useful for cooking family-size meals. I found out that my concerns about cooking dovetailed with John's concerns about heating our house.

My Family

John and I are very close to our families. Even though we live several states away from our parents, we always try to get together around the Holidays each year. It's a big group—aunts, uncles, cousins—and a lot of fun. It's difficult to think about, but with all the unknowns going into the year 2000, I'm not sure it would be a good idea to be traveling so close to the end of the year. We've been talking with our families about the year-2000 problem, and it looks like we're going to have our get-together at Thanksgiving instead.

Changing the date of our family reunion took some convincing with my parents. Because they weren't familiar with the year-2000 problem, they didn't understand our concerns at first. One good thing came out of the discussions though. Now my parents have decided to make some year-2000 preparations—a big relief for me. Because they live quite a distance away, I've been worried about their welfare. I feel confident now that Mom will take precautions with her health problems.

John and I have urged Mom to talk with her doctor about the impact the year-2000 problems may have on her healthcare. I know her physician will do whatever he can to make sure she has the medications she needs. John and I have told her that if her insurance company won't pay for additional medications, we will help her out.

John—My Thoughts

Just as Terry has been concerned with the food supplies, I wanted to make sure our family would be warm should we encounter power outages. I had a meeting with the contractor who is building our house yesterday. We discussed the various options and settled on a wood-burning stove in the family room instead of a fireplace. Some of the new models are really nice looking and will be much more efficient in providing heat than a fireplace. And the flat surface can double as a cook top. Of course, we've decided to stock up on warm blankets and other emergency supplies, such as candles, flashlights and batteries.

My Work

Since I'm in sales, I travel a lot. With the year-2000 problem, there are many things that could happen in my type of work that are beyond my control. Many of my customers are overseas where year-2000 concerns are not as well understood or are not high priority. But I'm focusing on the areas that I can control. Since it appears that overseas travel may be undependable for a while, I'm trying to schedule my international trips before November 1999. In November and December, it will be domestic travel only! And though I know my travel agent prefers to use electronic ticketing, I'm going to insist on hardcopy tickets for a couple of months. When the New Year rolls around, I'll be home. I've decided to take my vacation during the first two weeks in the year so that I won't have to travel until any reservation and scheduling, or other problems are worked out.

Last month when I was in Southeast Asia, I tried to use a credit card with a 2001 expiration date, and it was rejected. Since I had just used the card in the States, I suspect that the problem was not with the credit card company. I had another card with a 1999 expiration date—and it worked. Boy, did I luck out. Later, I discussed the problem with my supervisor and from now on out, I'll be issued a cash advance for travel.

I've noticed that my passport expires in June of 2000. I'm thinking it might be wise to get it renewed sooner rather than later. And since there will probably be a number of other people with the same idea, I intend to apply for my new passport early in 1999.

I'm very pleased that my company is taking year-2000 preparedness seriously. Some of our normal ways of doing business could be at risk. Our information systems people have been busy making sure that all of the computers we rely on will be compliant, both the ones in the office where the inventory and customer databases are maintained and the laptops like the one I carry with me on trips.

While I am travelling, I try to keep in touch with Teresa and the kids, calling every evening when I'm in the US, and as often as possible, considering the time differences, when I'm overseas. From what I have read about the year-2000 problems in telecommunications, I'm afraid that I may not always be able to make that *goodnight* call. The best solution I could come up with was to have long distance accounts with several major companies. Hopefully, one of them will be working. Of course, email is another possibility, but it just wouldn't be the same as hearing my kids' voices.

The Last Word

Working together has helped make preparation for the year 2000 manageable. While we have some decisions yet to make, we're feeling pretty good about the plans we've made so far. Even though it's going to cost us some money, the peace of mind knowing our children are going to be safe and warm makes it all worthwhile.

Chapter 15

JoAnn and Derek and the Year 2000

About JoAnn and Derek:

- Single working mother
- Non-traditional college student with loans
- Lives in a high-rise apartment
- Reliant on public transportation

JoAnn—My Thoughts

As I consider the potential for year-2000 problems, my main concern is for Derek, my six-year old son. Since I don't have family close by, I need to be as self-reliant as possible. Although my ex-husband, David, isn't as worried about year-2000 consequences as I am, we both agree that Derek's welfare is our top priority.

Our Lifestyle

I decided to involve Derek in my year-2000 preparations. One of the things we had fun doing was pretending the power was out and coming up with solutions for the problems that surfaced. I think that one of the advantages of making it into a game was that it helped prepare Derek for a power outage, should one occur. Although we couldn't turn off the power to the apartment, we could simulate a power outage manually. We unscrewed light bulbs just enough for them not to work and unplugged appliances, lamps and the television. Derek missed some of his favorite television shows, especially cartoons like Barney, that he watches almost everyday. It became clear right away that I would need to have some things on hand to keep him occupied if we lost power.

I found out that our phone, a cordless one, wouldn't work at all without electricity. It wasn't that we lost phone service. It's that the base unit required power to transmit the message to the handset. I decided to buy a regular phone for the jack in my bedroom. I've been through power outages before when the phones continued to work even though the electricity was out.

Next, Derek and I pretended that we couldn't use our stove and oven and discussed what we would do to replace them. Derek was fine with peanut butter-and-jelly sandwiches, but I knew I would tire of them as a steady diet pretty quick. I remembered that my Aunt Marge use to use something called canned heat under her fondue pot, so I stopped at a sporting goods store and found a nifty little one-burner stove that operates on the same principle. At least I'll be able to heat up a can of soup.

Since I live in a rather small apartment, I don't have much room to store extra food and water supplies. Plus, I've never been very interested in cooking elaborate meals. On most days I'm pretty worn out by the time Derek and I get home. It's just so much easier to fix something quick, like a boxed macaroni-and-cheese dinner from the grocery store. But I want to be prepared, so I have set aside space on two shelves of my linen cupboard to stock extra foods, mostly canned and dried goods such as spaghetti sauce and pasta, and some of the newer packet foods which contain stews and curries. David will store more food at his home in case my limited supply isn't sufficient, which is good as Derek visits David every other weekend. I want to know Derek will have plenty of food wherever he is should there be problems.

Because my budget is limited, I'm going to spread my purchases over a number of months, and I'll be careful to select only items that we ordinarily use. But there was one problem that stumped me for awhile. If the power goes out, how could I keep milk on hand for Derek? Finally I found a solution. I discovered you can buy packaged milk that can store for almost a year. I found the packages next to the powdered milk and canned milk on the grocery store shelf. Derek says it tastes just fine.

I've been a little concerned about living in a high-rise apartment. At first I was worried about the stories I heard of elevators stopping dead after the year 2000. But the building manager in our high-rise explained that our elevators use trip counters, not dates, to determine if maintenance is needed. And the elevators are not tied to any kind of management system, so there shouldn't be a problem.

Still if the power goes out, I would have a difficult time getting up and down twelve flights of stairs with a six-year old in tow. So David and I have worked out a contingency plan. If the power is out more than 24 hours, David will come get us. In the meantime, Derek and I will have fun reading bedtime stories by candle light. My mother has told me that she will be giving us down comforters as an early Christmas present, so altogether, we will should stay warm and cozy.

My Job and School Records

I rely on public transportation to get to work and school. It just isn't feasible for me have a car, and I couldn't afford to pay for insurance and parking anyway. I am a little concerned that the year-2000 problem will affect the public transportation system. Luckily, school will be out for me and Derek during the holiday period, so I won't have to worry about either of us missing school. I do worry about getting to work though. The company I work for is typically open for business right up to Christmas Eve and then we start back to work the day after Christmas. Although we get New Year's Eve and New Year's Day off, we will be expected to begin working on Monday, January 3rd, 2000, bright and early.

It seemed to me that this wasn't my problem alone. I felt that the company I work for should also be concerned about transportation problems, as many of my co-workers use public transportation, too. So, I decided to talk with my supervisor about my concerns. She was impressed that I knew so much about potential year-2000 problems and told me she would be talking with her managers about contingency planning. Though she doesn't have any answers now, she expects the company will have to address this issue at a higher level as we get closer to the year 2000. January isn't a very busy time for my company, so I'm hoping we will get an extra few days off, just in case there are transportation problems.

I have done the standard things about saving checking and savings account statements and the like. But one thing that recently occurred to me was the importance of collecting my school records. I have a student loan that helps pay for my tuition. I plan to store paper copies in a safe place. I'm also going to keep current transcripts of all my courses and grades. I don't want to have to repeat any courses because of a computer glitch.

The Last Word

Although my needs aren't extensive right now, I learned that there are lots of options in dealing with what problems I might face. The most important thing I learned was that it was possible for me to be affected, *and* that I could find my own solutions to deal with potential problems.

Chapter 16

Commonsense and the Year 2000

As you are well aware after having read this book, the year-2000 problem will have a significant impact on many aspects of our lives and on the institutions and services we have come to take for granted. However, as you will also have learned by now, there are a lot of things you can do to help prepare yourself and your family for whatever problems you may encounter when the year 2000 arrives. Many of the tips and solutions for dealing with the year-2000 problem are commonsense. But, more often than not, commonsense is the first thing to disappear when we get scared.

Your mission, should you choose to accept it, is to continue applying commonsense to the areas in your life where year-2000 problems could arise. Because the scope of the year-2000 problem is broad, it is impossible for this book to address all the areas that could be affected. However, you now have an expanded understanding of the year-2000 problem and its *modus operandi*. With this knowledge, you can continue to apply commonsense in ways to minimize, offset, or even negate other year-2000 problems.

You have already made a choice to begin using commonsense—making the decision to read this book was a good start. Now, it is important to keep listening, learning, and questioning. People make decisions based on the information they have available. For this reason, it is crucial to keep gathering information in order to make sound decisions—decisions you can feel good about.

Good luck and best wishes! Happy New Year, and happy New Millennium.

Appendix A

Sources of Energy for Electric Generation Percentage Total of Electric Utility Industry by state and energy source

State/Region	Coal	Fuel Oil	Gas	Nuclear	Hydro	Other
Total United States	57%	2%	9%	22%	11%	0%
Maine	-	8%	-	67%	25%	0%
New Hampshire	21%	5%	-	64%	9%	-
Vermont	-	0%	-	82%	15%	3%
Massachusetts	41%	22%	16%	19%	1%	-
Rhode Island	-	2%	98%	-	-	-
Connecticut	15%	33%	6%	40%	3%	3%
New England	23%	17%	12%	41%	6%	1%
New York	20%	9%	13%	34%	25%	0%
New Jersey	29%	3%	12%	56%	-1%	-
Pennsylvania	58%	2%	0%	39%	1%	-
Middle Atlantic	43%	4%	6%	38%	9%	0%
Ohio	90%	0%	0%	10%	0%	-
Indiana	99%	0%	0%	-	0%	-
Illinois	50%	1%	1%	48%	0%	0%
Michigan	70%	1%	1%	28%	1%	-
Wisconsin	75%	0%	1%	20%	3%	1%
East North Central	76%	0%	1%	22%	1%	0%
Minnesota	65%	2%	1%	29%	2%	1%
Iowa	85%	0%	1%	12%	3%	0%
Missouri	84%	0%	1%	13%	2%	0%
North Dakota	89%	0%	-	-	10%	-
South Dakota	20%	0%	0%	-	79%	-
Nebraska	59%	0%	1%	35%	6%	0%
Kansas	75%	0%	1%	21%	-	-
West North Central	75%	0%	1%	17%	6%	0%
Delaware	52%	15%	33%	-	-	-
Maryland	63%	3%	1%	27%	6%	-
District of Columbia	-	100%	-	-	-	-
Virginia	49%	1%	2%	47%	1%	-
West Virginia	99%	0%	0%	-	1%	-
North Carolina	62%	0%	0%	33%	4%	-
South Carolina	40%	0%	0%	37%	3%	-
Georgia	64%	0%	0%	30%	5%	-
Florida	45%	16%	21%	18%	0%	-
South Atlantic	60%	4%	6%	28%	2%	-
Kentucky	96%	0%	0%	-	4%	-
Tennessee	63%	0%	0%	26%	11%	-
Alabama	64%	0%	0%	26%	10%	-
Mississippi	42%	4%	22%	32%	-	-
East South Central	70%	1%	2%	25%	8%	-
Arkansas	56%	0%	7%	31%	6%	-
Louisiana	32%	0%	41%	27%	-	-
Oklahoma	67%	0%	28%	-	4%	-
Texas	49%	0%	37%	13%	0%	-
West South Central	49%	0%	34%	15%	1%	-
Montana	47%	0%	0%	-	53%	-
Idaho	-	-	-	-	100%	-
Wyoming	97%	0%	0%	-	3%	-
Colorado	94%	0%	1%	-	5%	-
new Mexico	86%	0%	9%	-	1%	-
Arizona	43%	0%	2%	41%	13%	-
Utah	96%	0%	1%	-	3%	1%
Nevada	69%	0%	21%	-	10%	-
Mountain	70%	0%	4%	11%	15%	0%
Washington	7%	0%	0%	5%	87%	0%
Oregon	4%	0%	3%	-	93%	-
California	-	1%	27%	30%	38%	4%
Pacific	4%	0%	12%	14%	68%	2%
Alaska	5%	7%	65%	-	22%	-
Hawaii	-	100%	-	-	0%	-
Alaska and Hawaii	2%	62%	26%	-	9%	-

Percentages may not add-up to 100% due to rounding and non-inclusion of miscellaneous power resources.

Source: Edison Electric Institute, Table 23, *Sources of Energy for Electric Generation by State and Energy Source*, 1996 Statistical Yearbook.

Index